PERFECT BALANCE

A YOUNG ATHLETE'S
GUIDE TO THE
WORLD OF
GYMNASTICS

JULIA KONNER, MPH, CHES

T0190858

an imprint of Ulysses Press
PO Box 3440
Berkeley, CA 94703
www.velopress.com

VeloPress is the leading publisher of books on sports for passionate and dedicated athletes around the world. Focused on cycling, triathlon, running, swimming, nutrition/diet, and more, VeloPress books help you achieve your goals and reach the top of your game.

ISBN: 978-1-64604-6-980
Library of Congress Control Number: 2024931676

Printed in the United States
10 9 8 7 6 5 4 3 2 1

Front cover design: Amy King
Interior photographs: © Isaac Hayes except page 11 © sirtravelalot/shutterstock
    .com; page 105 © Alex Emanuel Koch/shutterstock.com; page 173 © Juice Dash/
    shutterstock.com

Please note: This book has been written and published strictly for informational purposes, and in no way should be used as a substitute for consultation with health-care professionals. You should not consider educational material herein to be the practice of medicine or to replace consultation with a physician or other medical practitioner. The author and publisher are providing you with information in this work so that you can have the knowledge and can choose, at your own risk, to act on that knowledge. The author and publisher also urge all readers to be aware of their health status and to consult health-care professionals before beginning any health program.

To my parents for their endless support, energy, genes,
and approximately 2,500 hours of driving me to and from practice.

CONTENTS

INTRODUCTION

So you're a gymnast! This is your identity. Gymnastics has been your life for so many years, and you couldn't imagine your life without it—except...could you? I have been where you are, and it is no easy decision. Some days in the gym are grueling and feel pointless. Some days are just the opposite. You perfect a new skill, something you've been struggling with clicks, or you get over that fear that has been holding you back. Some days it is just nice being in the gym with your best friends because, let's be real, half the time you are going to practice just to hang out with your friends.

I get it, and I've been there too. I started gymnastics at five, when a friend's parents asked my parents if I wanted to go to a gymnastics class with their daughter. My parents didn't know much about the sport, but I was an active kid, so they thought, "Sure, why not? It'll wear her out and she'll sleep well afterward." Well, countless hours in the gym later, I can say that sometimes gymnastics helped me sleep better. And sometimes it was exactly what kept me up at night.

After taking classes and being one of the few children able to climb the rope, I was asked to move to the team. I competed in club gymnastics throughout high school, competed for my high school team, and then went on to earn a full athletic scholarship from a National Collegiate Athletic Association (NCAA) Division I school. I competed all four years in college and was voted team captain for my junior and senior years. So it's safe to say that I absolutely couldn't imagine what my life would have looked like without gymnastics. But there is something that should be said about the way the sport can take over your life.

Gymnastics doesn't start as a big commitment. For me, it was an hour-long class once a week, and then a couple of hours twice a week, and then by middle school and throughout high school it was five hours a day for five days a week. The hours and the time commitment sneak up on you until one day you realize that gymnastics is almost your entire life! Sometimes this is the best feeling, and sometimes it is the scariest thought in the world.

Although I competed for 16 years and have fond memories of the sport, I can't tell you how many times I thought about quitting or questioned why I was pursuing this sport. I remember many days after school being driven by one of my parents to practice (an hour away) while I was wondering, "What are my friends doing right now? Are they hanging out without me?" Or "I really don't want to have to do my dismount off the beam today because I'm so afraid—but I know I'll have to." These are just a few of the thoughts that I still remember, and I'm sure you have many similar ones.

In fact, during my senior year of high school, I received an offer from a Division I college to compete on their pole-vaulting team because gymnasts make great pole vaulters. At this time, mind you, I already had a gymnastics scholarship, and I was *still* considering it! I had done gymnastics most of my life, and maybe it was time to try something new—maybe this was a sign.

I chose to stick with gymnastics, and I'm glad I did, but this doesn't mean those questioning thoughts completely left my mind. When I'd have a bad day in the gym, sometimes I'd think, "If I were pole vaulting right now, then I wouldn't have just split the beam," or "If I weren't doing a sport, then I would have time to go see that new movie or go out with that cute guy."

All of these thoughts are relentless! But that is why I wanted to write this book and write this book for *you*. You, the one who is in love with your sport but also absolutely hates it at times. You, the one who wonders, "What else could be out there for me?" You, the one who may not love gymnastics any longer but wonders if the love will come back. You are not alone.

There is no right answer when deciding whether to stay in or leave the sport. My hope is that this book will show you that your thoughts are completely normal and that it will give you the space to process these thoughts. There is no one who truly understands everything that gymnastics requires from you—the time, energy, tears, and sometimes bruised or calloused skin—so please take your time with this book. You do not need to make any rash decisions. Give yourself the patience to sit with your thoughts.

Although I had wonderful coaches, teammates, and experiences while in gymnastics, I never had a mentor to provide guidance on the constant ups and downs. I hope that this book, coming from someone who has been exactly where you are, will provide mentorship for you. This book is intended for current gymnasts and their parents, who maybe didn't compete themselves but are curious about what is required by the sport or how to help their child trying to navigate this complex landscape.

This book takes an objective look at the many facets of gymnastics, so you will feel ready to make the decision to either continue or end your gymnastics journey. With that in mind, I divided the information in this book into three parts.

Part 1 looks at the benefits of the sport and why I still call it the best sport ever. We'll look at the mental side of gymnastics and how mental toughness affects every area of your life as a gymnast and beyond. We'll also look at the strength building that comes with the sport, the good habits you learn, and the coordination and confidence you develop. We will end with the social benefits of the sport and the lasting benefits of these friendships and relationships.

Part 2 looks at the downsides of the sport. This section could also be referred to as the "ugly truth" and digs into the time commitment, fears, body dysmorphia, perfectionist tendencies, and injuries that are just as much a part of gymnastics as the benefits.

Part 3 is intended to help you come to your decision. By this point, all the pros and cons of gymnastics will be laid out, and you will be able to determine which direction you are leaning. You'll learn about decision-making and how to make peace with your decision. For parents, you will look at navigating this from your perspective and the best way to support your child. This book is not intended to try to sway you in any particular direction. It is meant to be an objective look at gymnastics that allows you to reflect and come to your own decision.

Throughout the book you will see "Write It Out" sections and "Ask the Expert" sections. The Write It Out sections include prompts to help process your thoughts and better understand your mind. The Ask the Expert sections include direct quotes from interviews I had with experts in their various fields.

After looking at the best and worst parts of the sport (with space for processing), I hope that you can determine for yourself if you will continue to maintain the "perfect balance" that gymnastics requires, or if it is time to find your next passion. If you do want to continue, then I have provided advice on moving from club gymnastics to collegiate gymnastics and ways to earn an athletic scholarship. If it is time to move on from gymnastics, then I have provided some next steps, thoughts on quitting, and ideas on how to get rid of the negative stigma of that word.

This book is also interactive. You can write directly in it! Feel free to write in the pages about your own experiences, opinions, and thoughts as they come to mind. I am excited to take this journey with you. I hope to be a mentor and guide through this interesting, unique, and challenging time. Let's get started!

PART I

THE BENEFITS

MINDSET

"Life is not about how fast you run or how high you climb but how well you bounce."

—Vivian Komori
American businesswoman;
CEO and founder of The Broad Perspective

In this chapter, we are going to look at how gymnastics builds a special kind of mindset and set of skills for mental toughness. We will also look at what you can do to continue to develop this psychological edge. There is no success in this sport without some level of mental toughness, and I love that gymnastics helps to build it.

One of the best aspects of gymnastics is the mindset it forces you to have. If you've been doing gymnastics for at least a few years, then you know what I'm talking about. Gymnasts are *tough*. There is no doubt about that. And it doesn't happen by chance. To start, gymnastics teaches you to do the following:

- Reset after a setback
- Cope with failure
- Put in the work to increase success

RESET AFTER A SETBACK

I love the chapter opening quote by Vivian Komori; it is so fitting when it comes to gymnastics. When I think of every time I failed in gymnastics—every time I fell during a meet, split the beam during practice, or missed a release move on the bars—every single time, I got back up. Getting up was not fun, but I did it anyway! I learned how to bounce back because I needed to finish my routine or take my next turn.

In women's gymnastics, if you fall on the beam during a competition, then you still have three other events to complete. For men, if you fall on the rings, then you have *five* more events to complete! It is futile to harp on whatever you have just messed up. The only way forward is to pick yourself up and move on to the next thing. The ability to pick yourself up again and again is a big part of your training. I'm sure you've had times when you've fallen in practice or at a meet and simply given up. You're human and it happens. But I hope you realized that approach wasn't successful, and you chose to reset and keep moving the next time. Even elite and Olympic athletes make mistakes, both in the gym and during competition. Setbacks are inevitable, but you have the gymnast mindset, which allows you to let go and move on.

Write It Out

Following are some questions that you can ask yourself when you've had a setback. Whether the setback was within or out of your control, you have the ability to choose your next move. Take a look at the questions, and see how you would process the next steps:

1. What just happened?
2. Why did this happen?
3. Was there anything I could have done differently?
4. What can I work on or what are my next steps?

Here is an example of how you can think through these questions:

1. I fell on the floor during a state meet.
2. I went crooked on the roundoff and it threw off my double.
3. My coach keeps telling me to focus on pushing off from my other arm more so I don't go crooked, but I was nervous and forgot during competition.
4. Focus on that correction during practice more until I don't need to remind myself in competition, when I'm nervous and distracted.

These process steps can be used outside the gym as well. Consider this example:

1. I missed my project deadline.

2. I had a report due, so I spent too much time on that.

3. I could have broken up my time instead of focusing all my energy on the report.

4. Take time before a project starts to lay out the steps and break down the tasks so I can better manage my time.

Try it out for yourself! Think of a recent setback you've experienced, and answer these questions to help you let go of your mistake and take the next step forward.

1. What just happened?

_____

_____

2. Why did this happen?

_____

_____

3. Was there anything I could have done differently?

_____

_____

4. What can I work on or what are my next steps?

_____

_____

COPE WITH FAILURE

There is no way to avoid failure in gymnastics. The entire premise of the sport is to do "perfect" routines to get a perfect 10. But 99.9 percent of the time, that's not going to happen. So the only way to get around this is to either be a perfectionist (which is not ideal—we'll talk more about that in chapter 10) or to deal with failure. This is not easy, especially for the personality type of most gymnasts. That is where your training comes in.

There are very, very few (probably zero) days at practice when you don't fall or make a mistake in some way. In the gym, you may be falling because you are learning a new skill, or it could be a skill you've had for years but continue to fall on. I will also go out on a limb and say that you are probably not getting perfect scores on every event at every competition. This means that, by definition, you are "failing" on an almost daily basis.

But every time you fall, you try again and make adjustments (mental and physical). You persist. Constantly failing also means that you are constantly challenging yourself. It means that you can face failures and move on, and it means that you are learning from your failures. Being comfortable with failing and embracing mistakes and the lessons they contain is not only helpful in the gym but also incredibly useful in the "real world." Most people don't have this powerful "perseverance despite failure" training.

I like to think of failing as being one step closer to succeeding. Of course, there are times when this is easier to believe than other times, but trying to hold onto that mindset will work wonders in and out of the gym. In the realm of failure, there are a few key lessons that all gymnasts grow to learn.

FAILURE IS NOT THE END OF THE WORLD

Because there is so much falling and getting back up, you understand that the world goes on and that this is a normal part of the learning process. Failure builds resilience because you know that you have to keep trying, even when it is tough or frustrating. Studies show that more resilient people are happier[1] and more successful academically.[2] Resilience is built into your training and affects every part of your life, from your mental outlook to academic and professional success.

Grit

Another facet of resilience that I particularly like is something called grit. This is perseverance and moral resolve, which allows you to reach long-term goals despite obstacles.[3] Dr. Angela Duckworth, PhD, a psychologist at the University of Pennsylvania, has dedicated her research to studying grit and why some people are successful and some aren't, regardless of IQ or abilities. In her TED talk "Grit: The Power of Passion and Perseverance," which now has more than 13 million views, Dr. Duckworth talks about this research. Her team looked at a range of contexts, from which cadets would complete their training at the United States Military Academy at West Point, to who would win the Scripps National Spelling Bee, to which rookie teachers in tough neighborhoods would stay and demonstrate the best learning outcomes for kids, to which sales representatives would be the most successful in selling their product. After looking across these different areas, the most significant predictor of success was grit,[4] or the passion to achieve long-term goals. For example, when looking at which cadets would complete their training at West Point, they looked at everything from high school rank to SAT scores, leadership potential score (extracurricular activities), physical aptitude, and grit. It was this last quality that best predicted who would prove to be successful.

Now you're probably saying, "Okay, I understand what grit is, but how do I get it?" Gymnastics is a great start! Other researchers, such as Dr. Carol Dweck, PhD, from Stanford University, have found that the best way we know to increase grit is to have a growth mindset.[5]

So what is a growth mindset? It is the belief that the ability to learn is not fixed and can change with effort.[6] If people understand that the brain has the ability to change, then they tend to persevere more after failure. The growth mindset says that we can always improve; the fixed mindset suggests that we are born with our IQ, talents, and abilities and cannot change anything. Take a look at the following chart, which compares these two types of mindsets. Do you see yourself in one of these categories more than the other? Maybe you're a mixture of both. Use this chart to see where you are doing well and where you can improve.

Fixed Mindset	Growth Mindset
• Avoid challenges	• Challenges are opportunities
• Limited by failure	• Failure allows for growth
• Refuse critique	• Embrace critique
• Stick to what you know	• Try new things
• Threatened by others' success	• Inspired by others' success
• Focused on the end result	• Focused on the process
• Avoid unfamiliar things	• Try to get out of the comfort zone
• Talent is static	• Talent can be improved

Write It Out

Think about a situation when you followed a fixed-mindset approach. What was the outcome?

_____

_____

_____

Now think of when you were in a tough situation and followed growth mindset. What was the outcome?

_____

_____

_____

Finally, think of something that happens to you fairly often in the gym—for example, the way you accept a critique. Do you embrace it or get frustrated by it and take it personally? Do you doubt your talent and compare yourself to your teammates, or are you proud of the growth you've made? Gymnastics training teaches you that failure is a stepping stone to success, and using the growth mindset in practice, in competition, and in life allows you to overcome whatever obstacles are thrown your way.

PUT IN THE WORK TO INCREASE SUCCESS

I've always appreciated the fact that in gymnastics, when you put in work, you get better. This might sound obvious, but there are other sports that rely more on raw talent rather than building skills over time. Most sports rely on one or two skills: speed, strength, grace, strategy, power, flexibility, agility, and so on. Gymnastics, on the other hand, requires all these skills at essentially the same time. Additionally, these skills are often contradictory. For example, strong people usually aren't so flexible, and powerful people aren't usually so graceful; but in gymnastics, part of the training is improving and excelling in all of these different skill sets.

Maybe one or two of the skills comes naturally, but for the others, you have to dedicate more time to improving them. For example, I was always strong and powerful but struggled with flexibility and grace. I had to put in extra work to improve on my weaknesses, but I knew that if I did supplemental stretching and practiced my floor and beam choreography, then I would improve my flexibility and gracefulness. My weaknesses were not static; I just needed some additional time to improve on them. This took lots of time and mental stamina because these skills did not come naturally to me. The problem with working hard to get better is that it is *slow*! This can be frustrating. Sometimes you feel that you worked hard at practice today and the week before and the month before that...so why isn't anything changing? Don't worry, it will! But having that impatient mindset is like watching water boil; the more you watch it, the longer it seems to take.

PATIENCE

Like it or not, gymnastics teaches you that even after hard work, the reward may still take some time to arrive. Skills aren't developed within a day or a week. It takes awhile to progress from the pit to the tumble track to the mats to finally putting a skill on the floor. Even once you have a skill on the floor or high beam, it takes even more time to master it. For example, when I was learning a shoot over on bars, I first practiced for months going from a single bar to a pile of mats. This was not only to learn how to move my body correctly but also to overcome my fear. Eventually, I was able to move to the real bars, with a sting mat over the low bar, and then finally I felt brave enough to go from the high bar to the low bar with no mats. Even once I got the shoot over on real bars, I had to figure out how to go from catching the bar in a horizontal position to catching the low bar in a handstand. It took repetition after repetition with spots, moving mats around, and all sorts of drills to understand the movement, and then how to do it correctly, and then how to hit a handstand every time.

It's said that nothing worth having comes easily, and gymnastics is a testament to that. You have to put in time and more time until you can eventually say you have mastered that skill! Patience is not a skill that many people naturally have. But your ability to develop patience through your gymnastics training will allow you to excel in the future.

Related to practice and patience, focus on these three steps:

Step 1. Focus on what you can change.

Step 2. Be consistent about that change.

Step 3. Stay present.

It can be hard to see that patience, as well as putting in the time and work, are the keys to increasing your success. Try the exercise that follows to see how you have improved through patience, consistency, and hard work.

Write It Out

Write down a time when you persisted and eventually achieved your goal.

_____

_____

_____

Remember, natural talent can get you only so far, especially when skills get harder or scarier as you move up levels. I've often seen extremely talented gymnasts face a challenge for the first time and not know where to start. The idea of hard work or overcoming is somewhat foreign to them. Going back to Dr. Angela Duckworth's study, she found that grit was unrelated to talent and sometimes even showed that as talent increased, grit decreased.[7] We'll get into talent more in the next section where we discuss mental toughness.

MENTAL TOUGHNESS

MENTAL TOUGHNESS AND YOU

Karen Cogan, the lead sports psychologist for the US Olympic and Paralympic Committee, put together the following list for mentally tough athletes.[8] Take a look. How many of these qualities describe you? Check them off as you go!

Mentally tough athletes:

☐ Set goals and have detailed plans to track and reach their goals

☐ Compete primarily against themselves

☐ Take ownership of their attitude and behavior

☐ Pursue excellence, not perfection

☐ Have intrinsic motivation

☐ Hold intensity/passion for their sport

☐ Invest energy, push themselves toward improvement, and persevere through difficulties

☐ Work to understand the process of what it takes to improve/ excel in their sport

☐ Bring a positive attitude to the team environment

Frankly, I was never the most talented gymnast in the gym or at the competitions. Did I win countless competitions, win Eastern Nationals, and earn a full-ride scholarship? Yes. And do you know why? I like to think of it as my secret weapon: mental toughness! There was also a lot of hard work involved... but you get the idea. Although numerous teammates and other athletes were much better than I was at the sport, I still excelled because I knew how to mentally cope with setbacks and failure. Every time I landed a pass short on the floor, missed a Gienger, or ran straight into the horse (this actually happened during a competition!), I picked myself up and moved on to the next skill or event.

I remember many times when a teammate fell off the beam even during a meet, and the entire rest of the meet was a wash because she couldn't mentally recover after that first setback. She felt defeated and let that feeling take over her mind and body. She essentially gave up because of one mistake. Although that one mistake isn't trivial, don't you think it's better to fall, get back up, and continue to have a great rest of the meet? The best part of gymnastics is that you can fall off the beam and still win at the bars, floor, and vault!

Mental toughness gets you through situations like that. There are countless definitions of mental toughness. My favorite is from cyclist Christiana Bédard-Thom, who says that mental toughness is "a psychological resource that helps you to achieve challenging goals when faced with a stressor that puts your success in doubt."[9] This definition relates so much to gymnastics and fits well with the quote at the beginning of the chapter. Success in gymnastics is determined not only by how talented or athletic you are but also by how well you bounce back after you get knocked down. There are countless ways to be knocked down—most commonly, falling, injuries, or fear—which then can lead to discouragement or self-doubt. The key here is having a mental toughness mindset and telling yourself, despite what just happened, "I will still succeed."

You of all people know how much mental toughness this sport requires. Not only are you doing dangerous, highly technical movements that could easily lead to injury, but also in competition you are doing all this with a smile and making it look easy! This doesn't even take into account the times that you are practicing or competing with a lingering injury or general discomfort. All these things require mental toughness.

Getting up every time you fall and trying the skill again and again, that is mental toughness. Overcoming the fear of practicing a skill, that is mental toughness. Walking into the gym every day, even when you are tired or have had a long day at school, that is mental toughness. Getting back up after a bad fall, that is mental toughness. These are experiences not many people have to face in their lifetime. Yet you do so on a weekly, maybe even daily, basis. You are awesome.

MENTAL TOUGHNESS AS A LIFE SKILL

This mental toughness mindset—being able to bounce back after being brought down so many times—is a life skill that can be applied to countless areas of your life and will truly set you apart from others. For example, maybe you get a bad grade or do poorly on a test. But then your experience with mental toughness in gymnastics kicks in, allowing you to let go of that negativity and move on to the next thing. What's done is done. Now you have to focus on what you can control. You take that bad grade in stride and study harder for the next test.

The same mindset also sets you apart once you enter the workforce. I remember getting a critique from my boss on the first report I wrote in my first "real" job. The report (which I had spent weeks writing) was covered in red lines, corrections, and notes. My initial thought was, "I've done a terrible job." Then I took a step back and thought about how all the corrections were there to make sure my next report was better. In the same way that your coach critiques your every turn to make you a better gymnast, my boss was editing and commenting on my report to make me a better writer. It wasn't a personal attack. I hadn't done a bad job. It was constructive criticism.

Not everyone will be able to bounce back or take criticism as well as you do. You will be able to receive a critique from your boss and respond positively because you won't take it personally. You'll listen to what your boss says and then move on. Although others at work may be bogged down by any comments or criticism, you can take a critique, learn from it, and then get better. This mental toughness will serve you well for the rest of your life.

COMPETING UNDER PRESSURE

All the hours spent training in the gym are to best prepare you for the competition floor. But if you can't compete under pressure, then having the best routine in the world won't matter. Feeling pressure can sometimes lead to a panic cycle, which follows.

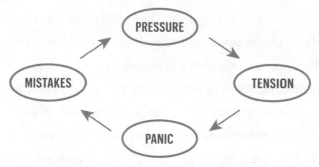

But you are a seasoned competitor, and you aren't fazed by pressure or difficult circumstances. You are conscious of your breathing, and you rely on your training and muscle memory to perform at your best, no matter what the environment. As an athlete, and a gymnast in particular, you have specific training to be successful under pressure that not many people ever receive, especially not at your age. Being able to perform under pressure is a life skill that will benefit you everywhere, from test taking and making presentations, to public speaking, interviews, and more.

Okay, so you have the training to remain calm under pressure, but you may be thinking, "Wait a second. I still get stuck in the panic cycle. What can I do?" This is another time when mental toughness comes in to help. Mental toughness allows you to be unshakable and remain focused when something goes wrong, even if there is chaos around you. So how do we increase our mental toughness to be our best when in the spotlight? Let's get into it!

BUILDING MENTAL TOUGHNESS

When I say that being mentally tough was my secret weapon, I don't mean that this quality was completely innate. I had to work at it constantly. All athletes, especially gymnasts, are more mentally tough in general. But just like any skill, mental toughness can *and should* be improved upon. Following are a few ways to improve your mental toughness.

Make mistakes and then choose to move on. You've probably heard this many times: don't dwell on your mistakes. Instead, bounce back. In gymnastics, mistakes are inevitable. There is no getting around that. But the choice is yours as to how to react to your mistakes. When they happen, think about them to understand what went wrong, and then make the conscious choice to move on. I understand that this is easier said than done, but the more you practice this, the more natural and automatic it will become.

Stay levelheaded, even in success. It's easy to let your mind fly, whether something good or something awful has just happened. A quote that I think about often is from professional soccer star Heather O'Reilly, who said, "You can't let the highs get too high and you can't let the lows get too low."[10] Just as you don't want to dwell on every little mistake, you also shouldn't revel in your success forever. This can build up an expectation that you should be successful every time, so you start to think, "If I'm not winning, then I'm failing." This is not the mentality we are looking for when developing our mental toughness. Instead, we want to learn both from our successes and from our failures—and then keep working hard.

Refocus. As much as gymnastics creates a mental toughness mindset, you can't be on all the time. It is still important to have mental cues to bring yourself back when your mind starts wandering. For example, when you're on the beam or the bars, it is easy to think, "Don't fall, don't fall, don't fall!" But the only thing your mind is hearing is, "Fall." Instead, take the time to refocus and talk to yourself about more positive things, such as taking deep breaths or staying in the moment. The next time you're about to start an event, think, "Breathe," "Stay present," or "Focus"—whatever keeps your mind positive but still intent on the skills you're performing. When you're on the floor or the vault, you might want to focus on something more energetic or powerful, such as telling yourself, "Quick," "Tight," or "Power."

It's also easy to get caught up in focusing on the end result of success rather than what is happening right now. Instead of thinking about the skill you are showcasing, you may be thinking about the score you might get. This is unproductive and usually ends poorly. Instead, use the mental cues in the preceding paragraph to refocus on what you are doing now. You can't change the end result with your thoughts alone. All you can change is what you are thinking and doing in this moment.

I was almost always talking to myself when competing. I'd be counting my steps or just saying what I was doing to distract myself from having negative thoughts, such as, "Don't mess up!" At one point in my senior year of college, I was putting too much pressure on myself to have a successful season. I wasn't telling myself my normal cues, and I was focusing too much on the end result of success. Then I tried saying my normal cues, but I still kept falling on my beam series. Something had to change. I decided to start singing to myself instead— silently of course. I know it sounds a little wacky, but try something until it works. And guess what? It did! I had to fully distract myself by singing, but it allowed me to refocus my mind and get back to a place where I was present, had confidence, and most importantly, stayed on the beam.

Write It Out

Write down what you say or could say to yourself to keep your mind busy when you are nervous.

_____

_____

_____

FIND YOUR MOTIVATION

It may not seem like motivation and mental toughness are related, but I beg to differ. If you are relying on an external factor to motivate you—such as the prospect of winning a meet, beating a teammate, or proving something to your coach or parents—then your mental toughness will be only as strong as your motivator.

Let's say your motivation is to beat your teammate, and then you finally do. Although the win may feel great at first, you were actually only working to be slightly better than that person, rather than doing your absolute best. Or let's say you are trying to acquire a new skill because your parents said they'd buy that thing you've been wanting. Well, once you get the present, do you really care about the skill anymore? If you have internal, or intrinsic, motivation, rather than external motivation, then you will want to succeed and keep improving for yourself. Your mental toughness won't rely on other people or things; it will rely on your own self-improvement for self-fulfillment. Presents are always nice, but the best gift you can give yourself is long-term success, and that comes from your own will and drive.

ASK THE EXPERT: DANIEL MIRANDA

Daniel Miranda is the cofounder, CEO, and head coach of Gotham Gymnastics (in Brooklyn, New York). He shares how motivation is specific for each athlete.

"Motivation is dependent on many factors. It is our job as coaches to make sure we give the right type of workout based on where we are in the season and where the athlete is mentally. If an athlete is feeling a lot of pressure or anxiety, they won't have the motivation to execute their routines to the best of their ability. We also tell our athletes that it's okay to take a day off and modify the workout in order to best recover and want to come back to practice. Whatever gets them to a better place mentally will help their physical abilities and performance."

STAY POSITIVE

You may think that the "stay positive" mindset is overused, but it's popular because it actually works! Talking to yourself and visualizing your performance in a positive light can do wonders for your performance and mental outlook. You can't feel very mentally tough if all you hear in your head is how terrible you are. It is essential to keep your thoughts and self-talk positive to remain self-confident.

Let's look at some examples of negative versus positive self-talk. Anything sound familiar?

Negative Self-Talk	Positive Self-Talk
• I can't do anything right. • I can't believe I fell on that really easy skill. • Don't mess this up like you always do. • I'm never going to master this skill. It's too hard. • Everyone else is ahead of me. I'm so behind.	• This skill has been challenging for me, but there are so many other skills I'm really good at. • It's okay to make mistakes. I am in control of the rest of my routine. • I can do anything I set my mind to. • I have overcome struggles in the past, and I will overcome them again. I can do this. • Some skills come more easily to me than others, I am a great gymnast and I can do this.

Write It Out

What are some examples of positive self-talk you can use when training or in competition?

_____

_____

_____

It's pretty cool to see how gymnastics uses both success and failure to teach mental toughness, grit, and other valuable life lessons. You can continue to improve by always working toward a growth mindset rather than a fixed mindset. You are already way ahead of your peers!

Now that we have a good understanding of the mental strength required in gymnastics, let's look at the physical side in chapter 2.

CHAPTER 1 KEY TAKEAWAYS

1. Gymnastics provides a psychological edge to help you cope better with setbacks, stressors, and failure.

2. Using a growth mindset instead of a fixed mindset allows you to strengthen your grit and build perseverance.

3. Mental toughness is the ability to face setbacks and then bounce back.

4. The mental side of gymnastics is just as important as the physical side.

5. Improve your mental toughness through accepting failure, staying level-headed, and refocusing, as needed.

THE PHYSICAL SIDE

"Take care of your body. It's the only place you have to live."
—Jim Rohn
entrepreneur, author, and motivational speaker

When most people think of gymnastics, they think of how most gymnasts look: strong, toned, and fit. This physique, as you know, does not come by chance. Hours are spent every day stretching and conditioning, which doesn't take into account how much strength is required to perform the skills on each event. If you've ever been away from the gym for more than a week or two, then you know the feeling of coming back, practicing, and waking up the next day with full-body soreness. When you're practicing every day, you aren't aware of how many little muscles are used with each movement, some that you probably didn't even know you had! For me, it was always total ab and core soreness from one day back on the bars after being on holiday. Few workouts can mimic gymnastics to work all the muscles that you use every day in practice.

In this chapter, we are going to cover how gymnastics builds that one-of-a-kind gymnast strength, sample exercises (with photos) to increase your strength and flexibility, the health benefits of strength, and how gymnastics builds body awareness, or spatial awareness.

STRENGTH BUILDING

There are countless benefits of building muscular strength through gymnastics. This includes being able to lift heavy things, knowing how to lift with the proper form to avoid injuries, and possessing a muscular physique that will stay with you for the rest of your life. We are going to get into all these reasons and more! But first, let's start with why gymnasts are so darn strong.

HOW GYMNASTICS BUILDS STRENGTH

The movements and skills required in gymnastics require significant upper body, core, and lower body strength. The average person cannot flip around, hold an L-sit, or walk around on their hands. To be able to control your body to perform the correct movements and be powerful enough to flip your body around, you have to have full-body strength.

As you know, there is no secret formula for building this strength. Most strength building in gymnastics comes from bodyweight exercises. Although using weights and resistance bands is also common, it often surprises people that gymnasts don't do much weight lifting (at least not at the club-gymnastics level). Then how are gymnasts so strong? Well, if you look at what is required for most routines—moving your body in precise movements while also keeping perfect form—then you see that a lot of strength is required. Just thinking about the level of strength required to perform difficult tumbling passes on the floor or watching any men's ring routine, you see how much strength is part of each routine.

Additionally, a good portion of practice every day is dedicated solely to conditioning. This conditioning ranges from bodyweight movements, such as pull-ups, rope climbs, leg lifts, levers, and core strengthening, to plyometric conditioning (jumping circuits) and block pushes, as well as specific gymnastics movements, such as handstand holds, press handstands, cast handstands, and so on.

Also, instead of adding more weight as you get stronger (as with regular weight lifting), as you progress through gymnastics levels, the skills become more difficult and require greater strength and body awareness. For example, on the floor at lower levels, you start with a roundoff back handspring, back tuck, or layout. By level 10, you are completing double backs or double layouts.

Over time, strength builds in your legs, arms, and back, which, along with the correct technique, gives you the power to perform more challenging tricks.

If gymnasts do use weights, it is usually for a specific purpose or area that needs to be strengthened. Let's say I needed to work on my forearm strength to improve my bar routine. I would probably use a simple weight attached to a stick and rotate the stick to raise the weight up and down to focus on this area. The following shows what this looks like:

It's not fancy, but this is one of the best ways to increase forearm strength, wrist mobility and strength, and it even works your core at the same time.

Weight exercise to increase forearm strength

Start with the rope completely unraveled. Hold your arms straight out in front of you (as shown). As you hold that position, shift your wrists to wrap the rope completely around the bar. Once the weight reaches the bar and there is no more rope, turn your wrists in the opposite direction (again, slowly shifting each wrist) to eventually release the rope until it is fully unraveled.

Try this a few times and see how much harder it is than it looks!

ASK THE EXPERT: STEVEN LOW

Steven Low is a former gymnast, a coach, and the author of *Overcoming Gravity: A Systematic Approach to Gymnastics and Bodyweight Strength* (2d ed.), *Overcoming Poor Posture* (with Jarlo Ilano), *Overcoming Tendonitis* (with Frank Skretch), and *Overcoming Gravity Advanced Programming*. He explains the need for slow and steady progress with strength and flexibility.

"Most people want to be strong and flexible and they want it now. But pushing yourself too aggressively without giving your body time to recover is doing too much. Focus on the long game in terms of strength and flexibility progress. As you know, most elite gymnasts take 10 to 15+ years to get to their level, so improving strength over time with technique training is going to take time. Be patient and relish the slow but steady gains."

Let's look at a few areas that build strength.

STRETCHING

The first way gymnastics allows you to build muscle is all that stretching at the beginning (and end) of practice. Stretching warms up and mobilizes the body, as well as strengthens your joints, creating strong connective tissue, which provides the foundation to put on muscle. Stretching and weight lifting also cause micro-tears in your muscles. During rest or recovery, your body responds to these micro-tears by repairing the muscle fibers, allowing them to grow back bigger and stronger.

I lift

Following are some examples of good warm-up movements that both stretch and strengthen your muscles:

- I, Y, and H lifts
- Weighted wrist lifts
- Banded pull-downs

Y lift

The I, Y, and H lifts are shown to the right. For the I lift, lie on your stomach and lift your arms (while keeping your head on or close to the ground) straight up. Your body should look like the letter *I*. For the Y position, your body is

H lift

in the same place, but lift your arms slightly wider than with the I. Your body should now look like the letter *Y*. For H, keep your body in the same position, but bend your arms and then lift up.

Another great movement is weighted wrist lifts. The movement also looks easy, but if you do enough, then you will feel the burn!

Sit on a panel mat or block where you can rest your forearm on your legs.

Hold the weight (as shown) and raise the weight up and down 20 to 25 times. Make sure to move only your wrist. Using other muscles or body parts to lift the weights takes away from the wrist strengthening of this movement.

If your current weight is too easy, then grab a heavier weight or add on repetitions.

You can also do this movement by turning the weight vertically and then lifting up and down or slowly and inten-

Weighted wrist lift

tionally twisting your wrist.

Another option is flipping your hand so your palm is facing the ceiling and holding the weight. Lift your hand so the weight moves up and down to strengthen your forearm.

A banded pull-down is when you wrap a band around the bar and then stand two to three feet away from the bar. Make sure there is tension in the band, then grab the band while standing in a hollow position. With straight arms, pull the band down until it reaches your upper legs. Do this 15 times while thinking about strengthening your core and building shoulder strength.

BUILDING FOUNDATIONAL STRENGTH

Gymnastics also builds strength through some foundational strength exercises. Although they are common, doing them on a regular basis provides a foundation for functional strength. A few examples follow (in no particular order):

- Push-ups
- Pull-ups
- Dips
- Leg lifts
- Hollow holds
- Hollow rocks
- Lunges
- Legless rope climb

In addition to these different ways that gymnastics builds strength, one of the main reasons gymnasts are so strong is simply the amount of time that they dedicate to training. You're probably working out as much as five hours a day. Even when you are working on events rather than conditioning, you are training (exerting force on) your muscles and strengthening them. I know gymnastics takes so much of your time (we'll talk about that in chapter 6), but not many people get to spend so much of their lives dedicated to getting stronger and fitter. Although it may feel like way too much time spent on conditioning now, many people would love to be able to spend even an hour or two working on their strength. And you get to do it almost every day!

Write It Out

Think about your gymnastics strength. Write down your favorite part of being strong.

_____

_____

_____

FLEXIBILITY

Flexibility is just as much a part of the physical side of gymnastics as strength. You spend countless hours every week dedicated to improving your flexibility. Flexibility training includes stretching not only the hip flexors (the most common stretch to improve leaps) but also the shoulders, wrists, back, and ankles. Having all-around flexibility makes your gymnastics look better, but also decreases the likelihood of injury.

Many hours are spent getting your splits down on the floor or with an elevated foot. Hip flexor flexibility is to improve your leaps. Other types of flexibility, such as shoulder or wrist flexibility, are useful for clean handstands, for skills on bars (eagle grip giants), and to prepare your shoulders and wrists for the force of floor and vault tumbling. Having greater flexibility in the shoulders, wrists, back, and ankles allows them to tolerate being pushed beyond their regular limits.

Sometimes great strength counteracts flexibility and vice versa. I was a perfect example of great strength and poor flexibility. You may be the opposite, or you may be lucky enough to excel at both! Either way, you get to dedicate 20 to 40 minutes (maybe more) a day to both strength and flexibility. Very few sports allocate so much time to these two seemingly contradictory exercises. Don't get me wrong, I dreaded stretching time and was certainly one of the least flexible in the gym, but even being among the least flexible in the gym, I was still the most flexible in my class, which I always enjoyed. I had to spend double the amount of time stretching as my teammates to be half as flexible. Frustrating? Yes, but there were other areas that came more easily to me than to them.

Stretching is not something that adults spend enough time focusing on. Adults also often don't know which stretches are good for which muscles. Even though being stretched every day is not easy, it is something that you are an expert in. This will help you to continue to stretch as you get older, which means you'll have less chance of injury.

Greater flexibility enhances your range of motion, reduces your muscle tension, and improves your posture. Additionally, boosting your flexibility and mobility allows for quicker recovery because it increases blood flow and reduces muscle tension.

ASK THE EXPERT: DR. NOLAN MERKER, PART I

Improving flexibility can sometimes feel like the bane of your existence as a gymnast. Dr. Nolan Merker, PT, DPT, is a former Division I athlete and current physical therapist (married to a gymnast) who shares his insights on using a technique called proprioceptive neuromuscular facilitation (PNF) to improve flexibility.

"PNF uses muscle activation of the same or opposite muscles contracting and relaxing to increase your range of motion. To improve your split using PNF, you need to lengthen your hamstring (back of your leg) by contracting and then relaxing it. You can also contract your quad muscle (front of your leg) and then relax it.

"To put these ideas to work, first get into your split position (if you are not all the way down). Sit in your split for a few moments. To start PNF, think about pushing down the top of your front leg (at your quad) and at the same time pressing the bottom of your back foot into the ground. Hold that squeeze for 10 to 15 seconds and then go back to your normal split. You should be able to get a little lower in your split. Repeat this a few times and see if there is improvement."

HEALTH BENEFITS OF STRENGTH AND FLEXIBILITY

Now that we've looked at how gymnastics builds your strength, let's look at the health benefits of being strong and flexible both today and in the future.

We know that being stronger and more flexible helps improve your gymnastics, and that doing gymnastics makes you stronger and more flexible, but how does this training help with everyday life and life after gymnastics?

Stronger Bones

First, gymnastics strengthens your bones. Think about the weight-bearing exercise of practice, which includes running, jumping, flipping, twisting, and landing. Consider resistance training with weights and bands. And reflect on the uneven, squishy, and foam surfaces that you bounce around on. These various exercises you do and surfaces you practice on exert force on your bones, which makes them produce more bone tissue, which increases your bone density. Greater bone density is helpful both now (for stronger bones) and also as you get older (to prevent osteoporosis, which is the weakening of the bones). Stronger bones mean they are less likely to break! Additionally, between the ages of ten and eighteen, you are developing the skeleton that will last you for the rest of your life![11] A strong physical foundation helps at every age to prevent bone breakage, stay fit, build muscle, and have better posture. Remember that bone strengthening is a cycle.

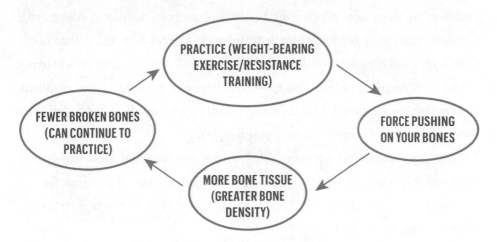

As you can see in the strength cycle, you are putting force on your bones during practice, building bone density, which means bones are less likely to break. This means you can keep training and the cycle continues.

On the other hand, flipping around isn't the only way to strengthen your bones. There are plenty of everyday weight-bearing exercises that build strong bones. These include walking, running, dancing, jumping rope, and racket sports (tennis, squash, pickleball, and so on). For resistance training, you can use weights, bands, or even just your bodyweight to do push-ups or pull-ups. Finally, for better balance, there is tai chi, yoga, or even standing or shifting your bodyweight from leg to the other.

In addition, flexibility is beneficial to allow you to move more easily at this age, as well as ease of movement when you are older.

You may be thinking that although it's great to avoid breaking bones, there are plenty of other ways to get hurt in gymnastics. Well, there is quite a bit of research about how being strong and flexible prevents all sorts of injuries. Let's check it out.

Prevents Injury

Not only does resistance training increase bone strength, but also it increases the strength of ligaments, tendons, joint cartilage, and connective tissue.[12] Ligaments, tendons, joint cartilage, and connective tissue are what keep your skeleton in place and allow your bones and muscles to move. Along with strengthening your bones, strength training reinforces everything that holds your bones and muscles together, which could break or tear if they aren't strong enough. Strength building makes sure ligaments, tendons, joint cartilage, connective tissue, muscles, and bones are all in alignment, which allows for fluid movement of muscles, thus preventing injury.

In particular, a strong core helps to prevent back injuries, which is a common injury in gymnastics. Your core is the front anchor of the spine. Strong core muscles support the spine, so there is less strain on the back muscles, which means fewer injuries.

Finally, strength training helps correct any muscle imbalances. When you move or put stress on your body, complementary muscle groups work together. When one muscle group is stronger than the other, it creates muscle imbalances, which can lead to injuries. If we focus on strength training for the lesser-used muscles group, then that muscle group will be strong enough to work with the opposing group.

Flexibility training can also be helpful in preventing injuries through enhancing muscle elasticity and improving joint mobility. Muscle elasticity means your muscles are able to absorb force, so there is less strain on tendons and ligaments, thus avoiding muscle tears. Joint mobility means the muscles, tendons, and ligaments that surround your joints are more flexible and can move more freely, so there is less strain on your joints.

Better Balance

Being strong also leads to better balance. If your muscles are trained and fit, then they can react more quickly to a balance shift and prevent you from losing your balance. A strong core also holds your body in better alignment when you are doing tricks where your body is swinging or moving at the core. For example, on the beam, having a strong core helps to bring you back to balance. If your center of mass is away from the beam, then a strong core helps you stiffen to find your center of mass to stay on the beam. Being stronger also means being able to stay in control of what your limbs are doing to bring them back into alignment.

ASK THE EXPERT: DR. NOLAN MERKER, PART II

Dr. Nolan Merker, PT, DPT, a former Division I athlete and current physical therapist, shares why a strong core is essential: "For every force you put into the ground, there is an equal and opposite force coming back from the ground to you. These forces are transmitted through your core, so your core needs to be strong enough to maintain your stability. When you are jumping, landing, flipping, and so on, the forces you are putting into the ground (and that are coming back to you) increase drastically and thus demand more of your core. Especially with gymnastics, you are flipping and twisting in all different directions, which means forces are moving your center of mass from all different sides. With a strong core, you are prepared for any force and can land correctly, while resisting the momentum generated from flipping and twisting."

GYMNASTICS STRENGTH STAYS WITH YOU

One of the best parts of starting a sport like gymnastics so young is that while you are training, you are building a skeletal and muscular structure that stays with you your entire life. For example, because my body was developing while being pushed physically every day, I developed broad shoulders, upper body strength, and muscular legs. Although I still work out, it is much easier for me to grow and maintain muscle than someone who is starting from scratch. I have a skeletal and muscular structure that is more predisposed to being strong and putting on muscle compared with most people. Building all this muscle at such a young age creates a foundation to maintain strength and fitness for life.

Posture

Stronger muscles and bones also mean better posture. If your muscles and bones aren't strong enough, then they cannot support your back, so it can more easily become rounded and bent forward.[13] Poor posture is often associated with lower back pain and fatigue. There are countless benefits of having good posture. These include increased confidence, more energy, easier breathing, and greater productivity. Good posture from strength, combined with a mental awareness of your posture, are great ways to not only look better but also feel more confident and powerful.

Endurance

As you know, the longest routine in gymnastics is only 90 seconds. But you also know that floor routine feels like the longest minute and a half of your life, especially when you're exhausted. Those 90 seconds of work are intense and require a high level of cardio conditioning to increase muscular endurance, which is great for the heart. A lot of gymnastics conditioning, such as plyometrics and partner interval training (PIT), are high-intensity to increase endurance and make routines feel easier.

Endurance is often a struggle for gymnasts because the routines are so short. Improving endurance is all about rep range. Generally, any exercise in which you feel a burn is going to build endurance, so aim for 20 to 30 or more repetitions. Cardio endurance is also built through low-intensity, steady-state (LISS) cardio. This is a low-endurance workout over a long period of time. Examples are walking, swimming, or hiking. LISS workouts may sound quite different from the high-intensity endurance required by gymnastics routines. But Steven Low, author and former gymnast (and our chapter expert), shares that LISS is a great way to build cardio endurance by forcing your heart to pump strong and steady for 30 to 40 minutes at a time.

YOU KNOW WHAT WORKS

In addition to building a physically fit body from years of doing strengthening exercises, you now know exactly which exercises strengthen which muscles. You have a plethora of exercises to pull from, so you'll never be bored, and (most important) you know how to do all the movements with correct form to avoid injuries. Although there is an appeal to looking physically strong and fit, knowing how to build and maintain muscle is something that will benefit you for the rest of your life.

Knowing which exercises to do to work a specific muscle group is half the battle for most people! This is why many people have personal trainers. They need someone to tell them exactly what to do to work each muscle. You, on the other hand, already have a repertoire of exercises when you get to the gym. If you get to the gym and don't have a plan or know what to do, then you won't stay long. If you get to the gym and have a list of exercises and muscle groups to work on, then you will be more productive with your time and more likely to return.

DOWNSIDES?

As much as I loved being strong and beating the boys, I know looking "too strong" can also be viewed negatively. You may not want to be stronger than your boyfriend or you may think that your large shoulders look "manly." With all your muscle, maybe you have a stockier build than the other girls in your grade, and you just want to be skinny and not strong. Gymnasts tend to have stockier builds because it's easier to flip around if you have shorter limbs and stronger muscles. Think about Simone Biles, who is pure muscle at four feet eight, or Shawn Johnson, who is four feet eleven. There are certainly exceptions to the stocky build (Nastia Liukin or McKayla Maroney), but short and muscular often comes with the territory. I understand these downsides, and you're not alone in thinking like this. But when you look at the bigger picture of what being strong and fit does for a person's gymnastics, general health, and future fitness, I'd rather be strong.

WAYS TO IMPROVE STRENGTH

Even though you probably know loads of ways to get stronger, strength may be an area that you want to get even better in. Of course you have plenty of time in the gym to work on conditioning. Following are a few ways to build strength outside the gym.

ISOMETRIC STRENGTH EXERCISES

Isometric strength building involves holding positions without moving for a set amount of time.[14] These exercises can increase strength in targeted muscles, without neighboring muscles jumping in and helping you improve your endurance. Isometric exercises can be done almost anywhere and don't require much equipment. Some examples follow.

- L-hold on a bar, rings, beam, or parallettes
- Traditional plank, side plank, or reverse plank
- Hollow hold
- Superman hold
- Wall sit
- Glute bridge raise

This is the L-hold on parallettes. It is a fantastic core exercise, but also uses your legs and arms to stay in this strong, tight position.

Hold for 30 seconds to 1 minute, depending on your strength, while keeping perfect form!

L-hold

This is the glute bridge raise. You can do it with your feet flat on the ground, or on your toes for more of a challenge. Lift your hips to the ceiling, and then slowly lower your hips to the floor.

Glute bridge raise

As you lift, think about squeezing your butt to strengthen your hamstrings and booty!

For an additional challenge, place one foot on the ground and lift the other in the air. Raise your lifted leg up to the ceiling, and then lower your butt down.

You probably already know what a traditional plank and side plank look like, but have you ever tried a reverse plank?

Lie flat and then place your feet on a raised surface, such as a panel mat (as shown). Raise your butt off the ground and squeeze until you are holding the position shown.

Reverse plank

It may feel a little weird at first, but holding a reverse plank for 1 minute can be a great isometric strength-training challenge.

DYNAMIC STRENGTH EXERCISES

Dynamic strength training is the opposite of isometric exercises in that rather than holding positions, you go through a full range of motion. Here are a few dynamic strength exercises.

- Walking lunges
- Jumping lunges
- Squats
- Handstand push-ups
- Pull-ups

Along with dynamic strength exercises, using the rings is one of the best ways to build strength. Even though women's gymnastics doesn't include the rings as an event, they are still invaluable for a strength-building tool and are often included during conditioning. Why are rings so great? Well, as soon as you hop up on the rings, it becomes pretty clear. Because the rings hang down, they move while you are using them. Keeping the rings still requires core strength while doing the exercise requires upper body strength. Rings also often require a false grip, which increases forearm strength. Not only are there plenty of exercises to do on the rings, but also rings are quite portable, which means more strength training in more locations. Check out the rings exercises that follow, and see what you have already mastered.

- Pull-ups
- Dips
- Muscle-ups
- Ring rows
- Ring butterfly
- Ring support hold
- Ring push-ups
- Flies
- Triceps extension

CALISTHENICS

Calisthenics can be particularly helpful for gymnasts. Calisthenics is quite similar to gymnastics training in that it uses only bodyweight to gain strength and muscle. I know you know plenty of exercises, but just for fun, see if you can conquer these calisthenic moves as well. You'll seem very cool if you can do these.

- Pike hold
- Lever
- Reverse pull-ups

Pike hold

Lever

Reverse pull-ups

ACTIVE FLEXIBILITY

In addition to strength-building exercises, there are plenty of stretches for active flexibility. The exercises below warm up the body, help prevent injuries, and allow for more fluid gymnastics movements. While these exercises improve flexibility, just like strength training, there is always more to work on in terms of flexibility.

- Lunges or splits
- World's greatest stretch
- Shoulder stretch with pinkies touching
- Cossack squat
- Toe touch with mat or beam
- Shoulder rotations with stick or band
- German hang

World's greatest stretch

Shoulder stretch with pinkies touching

Cossack squat

Toe touch with mat

Shoulder rotations with stick

German hang

BODY AWARENESS

Apart from building strength and all the benefits that come from being strong and flexible, a very special skill that gymnastics cultivates is body awareness, or spatial awareness. I don't mean awareness of what you look like; I mean awareness of where your body and limbs are in space and where your limbs are relative to each other. It may surprise you that this skill is not something that most people have. Gymnastics is so technical and therefore requires you to know where every limb is at all times. Without that body awareness, it would be very difficult to know when the ground is coming in order to land on your feet. When a coach says to "keep your ribs in" or "point your toes" while you are flying through the air, you must know exactly where your ribs and toes are to be able to make that correction. Part of this awareness also comes from strength training. Think about all the handstands and hollow holds you've done. During both of those exercises, you are told to squeeze everything from your shoulders to your toes. This means you are thinking about what each muscle is doing and where all your limbs are relative to each other.

Looking specifically at handstands, this is probably one of the first skills you learn, and it starts your body and spatial awareness journey. Practicing handstands helps you feel the correct positioning to hit your handstands in practice routines, as well as in competitions. It also increases upper body strength and balance, as well as your body awareness. You get used to having your feet over your head, keeping your ribs in, and positioning your head properly. Knowing where all your limbs are relative to the rest of your body, as well as being aware of what to squeeze and when is incredibly helpful for every other activity you will do in your life.

For example, I remember learning how to wakeboard. I saw other people before me struggling. I was told to keep my feet in a certain position, hold my arms at horizontal above the water, and squeeze my core. With these simple directions, and because I was aware of what each limb was doing, I was able to stand up on the board on my first try. Although other learners were told the same thing, they couldn't quite understand how all their limbs had to work together if they were to stand up. Having the awareness of what muscles to squeeze and when allows your body to work together and be able to perform whatever challenges you encounter.

Gymnastics provides a physical foundation that is helpful in all sports. From strength to flexibility, balance, agility, and coordination, these are all skills that are fundamental to gymnastics, help in all other sports, and will keep your body healthy for many years to come.

CHAPTER 2 KEY TAKEAWAYS

1. Gymnastics mostly uses bodyweight exercises to build incredible strength, tone, endurance, and flexibility.

2. There are numerous health benefits of strength training, including stronger bones and joints, injury prevention, confidence, and lifelong fitness.

3. There are also numerous health benefits of stretching, including reduced muscle tension, improved posture, injury prevention, and quicker recovery time.

4. Gymnastics trains the mind and body in order to increase body awareness, or spatial awareness, which is necessary in gymnastics, as well as applicable to other sports and areas of your life.

5. Strength is never a finished task. There are plenty of ways to continue to grow in your strength and flexibility.

DEVELOPING GOOD HABITS

"All people are the same; only their habits differ."

—Confucius

Along with the mental side and the physical side of gymnastics, what differentiates most athletes, and gymnasts in particular, are the life lessons and habits they develop along the way. Practice is used to master gymnastics skills, routines, and strength; however, training also encompasses countless life lessons and skills, which become habitual. Here are a few of the most prominent:

- Time management
- Discipline
- Setting and achieving goals
- Commitment
- Hard work
- Facing failure
- Teamwork
- Humility
- Patience
- Courage
- Determination
- Respect
- Performing in front of others
- Leadership

TIME MANAGEMENT

We all get the same 24 hours in a day, but some people are able to use their time more efficiently than others. Time management is deciding how to organize and spend your time. Having good time management skills allows you to be more productive, focused, and (it is hoped) less stressed.

Time management is a skill that was most likely ingrained in you at a young age so that you could keep up with your demanding gym schedule, along with all your other commitments, including school, family, friends, and social activities. At first, you probably weren't even aware of how good your time management skills were. You just knew that in order to get everything done, you had to find ways to be as productive and efficient as possible.

When I think about my days in gymnastics, it seems that every minute was assigned to either school, gym, eating, or homework. Four days a week, I would wake up, go to school, ride to practice (sometimes doing homework in the car), practice until 8:30 p.m., get home at 9:30 p.m., do homework until I was finished, go to bed, and wake up to do the same thing again the next day. Whew—I'm exhausted just thinking about it! Although every day was a marathon, it taught me how to properly manage the limited time I had to devote to each activity. Some of these time management skills follow:

- No procrastination
- Prioritization
- Setting a schedule
- Making lists
- No multitasking

NO PROCRASTINATION

I learned early on that procrastination is not an option when your time is limited. As soon as I got home, I knew I had to get straight into homework, even if I was tired or didn't feel like it, in order to get enough sleep. Procrastination, or putting off a task, delayed my time in bed, and getting enough sleep has always been a great motivator for me. Although most of your friends have time to procrastinate by watching TV or scrolling through social media, you do not have that luxury, and therefore you are learning an invaluable skill.

But if procrastination is something you still struggle with, despite your busy schedule, then giving yourself a strict deadline can be used as motivation. If setting a deadline for yourself doesn't work, then try setting time limits for tasks. For example, set a timer for 15 to 30 minutes to complete a task within the allocated time. These are both ways to eliminate procrastinator tendencies and improve your time management skills.

PRIORITIZATION

Another time management technique is prioritization. If I had something due the next day, then I would prioritize the homework with a tight deadline over homework that wasn't due until the next week. If I had a project, then I would save that for my day off practice or for the weekend, when I wasn't on such a time crunch. You can also prioritize based on the time a task will take or based on its importance. Some people like to get quick tasks out of the way, and some like to face their most time-consuming task first.

EAT THE FROG

The expression "Eat the frog" was created by author Brian Tracy as a technique to avoid procrastinating.[15] It means get the worst or most important task out of the way, so you can move onto more enjoyable tasks. The next time you are struggling to feel motivated to start something, just think, "Eat the frog and be done with it!" Once the worst task is out of the way, everything else should seem easier—and it's one less task to face. Try repeating this every day to face your challenges and avoid putting them off.

SETTING A SCHEDULE

Gymnastics also makes you prioritize activities for the little bit of time you have on the weekend. Because Friday night and most of Saturday were spent in the gym, I wanted to make sure I got the best use out of the remaining time I had. Making schedules for my weekends helped me plan out each day to use every moment to the fullest. Especially if you know you have social or family obligations, creating schedules allows you to make the best use of any extra time that you can fit in.

MAKING LISTS

Something that was and is helpful when I'm feeling overwhelmed is creating lists. Lists lay out everything that needs to get done and allows you to clearly see what has been accomplished and what is left. There is also something very satisfying about checking items off a list.

NO MULTITASKING

Finally, in order to be most productive, avoid multitasking. Working on several tasks at once can feel like you are getting a lot done, but it actually slows you down because your brain is jumping around, not focused on the task at hand. To be most effective, focus on one thing at a time and check items off your list.

Having good time management skills will serve you well in school, college, your job, and life. You have experience avoiding procrastination. Instead, you prioritize tasks, set schedules, and make lists. Along the way, you avoid multitasking. All these skills allow you to be productive and efficient with the time you have and the tasks in front of you.

DISCIPLINE

Although it is well known that sports are a great way to build discipline, the discipline necessary to be a gymnast is in a class of its own. First, few if any sports require the same time commitment as gymnastics. It takes discipline to train for five hours a day and as much as 30 hours a week. You also learn discipline from showing up to practice every day at the same time, on time.

Next, there is a strict warm-up routine that is done in sync in order to build and demonstrate discipline. Once practice starts, it is common that there is no sitting allowed. Additionally, each skill you do requires total concentration and the ability to block out distractions. Even the practice of putting away mats or equipment after each event to make sure the gym is kept clean and in good order builds discipline.

Finally, you must be disciplined about the food you eat and the amount of sleep you get if you are to do your best at practice every day. Your superb time management skills, discussed in the preceding section, also require discipline. When you are on a strict schedule, you must have self-restraint in order to stay on track and complete all your tasks.

Having discipline in your life allows you to focus on and achieve your goals, while also being efficient and organized.

SETTING AND ACHIEVING GOALS

Gymnastics is all about setting and reaching your goals. For example, you can think of each skill you learn as a goal achieved; each level is another goal. You are constantly working toward the next achievable goal. You can have your short-term goals (within a week to a month), medium-term goals (within a few months), or long-term goals (within a year or more). You may have goals that are set many years in advance, such as making it to nationals or becoming elite. But the best way to attain your goals is to break them down into more manageable pieces. You can do that by making all of your goals SMART goals. SMART stands for the following:

Specific: Be specific with your goals. Maybe your goal is, "Get better at bars." This is very general. To make it more specific, you could say, "Get my giant" or "Learn XX release move." Having specific goals gives you a clear marker so you know exactly if and when you've achieved your goal.

Measurable: You have to be able to measure your goal. For example, if you say you want to be stronger, then that is a broad statement that doesn't give you a clear goal against which to measure the strength you're developing. Setting the goal of being able to do 20 pull-ups is a measurable goal of strength; you will know whether you have achieved it.

Achievable: Your goal should be realistic. It should certainly push you, but it should still be reasonable. For example, if you're in level 5, then it wouldn't make sense to set your goal to do a double back off the beam. It wouldn't be realistic or achievable because you would have to learn more skills before jumping to a double back. If you are in level 10 and already have a roundoff dismount but want to learn a double back, then that is a more achievable goal. In level 5, a long-term goal could be to learn a roundoff dismount.

Relevant: Your goal should be related to your life and meaningful to *you*. For example, you wouldn't set the goal to learn a new beam series if you already had one, since you only compete one beam series. Or you wouldn't set a goal that your parents or your coach said to achieve but you didn't actually care about. Your goals should come from you and be relevant to improving your gymnastics skill set.

Time-based: Your goal needs to have some sort of timeline or be time-sensitive. It is helpful to set a time frame for the achievement of your goal. For example, if your goal is to learn a new vault, then you could set this goal at the beginning of summer, with the end of the timeline in October, when you are starting to get ready for competition season. Setting a time frame can help motivate you, but it also allows you to schedule steps that you need to accomplish in order to achieve your goal.

Articulating your goals, making them SMART, and then executing them is a very important skill that can be applied to other areas of your life. Gymnastics trains you to think with a goal-oriented mindset. It's said that setting goals without a plan is just a wish. Don't wish it; make it happen.

Write It Out

1. What is a short-term (within a week to a month) goal you have?

_____

_____

_____

2. What is a medium-term *(within a few months) goal you have?*

_____

_____

_____

3. What is a long-term *(within a year or more) goal you have?*

_____

_____

_____

Now make it SMART:

Specific:

_____

_____

Measurable:

_____

_____

Achievable:

_____

_____

Relevant:

_____

_____

Time-based:

_____

_____

COMMITMENT

To commit to something means to dedicate yourself to that thing by investing your time and energy in it.[16] To achieve long-term goals, commitment is almost always necessary. Gymnastics teaches commitment first and foremost in the time commitment required of practice, conditioning, and competitions, as well as the energy commitment required of practicing so much. Additionally, moving from level 4 to level 10 takes many years and requires you to be committed to long-term success by facing the days, months, and years of hard work, failure, and success to reach the highest level. Commitment is an invaluable skill that is beneficial for school, work, friendships, relationships, and beyond. There will be many times when you don't like what you're doing, but you know how to stay committed in order to achieve long-term success.

HARD WORK

By doing gymnastics, you are choosing the path of hard work. Gymnastics is hard work and builds your capacity for more hard work because you experience so much pain and failure, and you need self-discipline to reach success. The Merriam Webster dictionary defines hardworking as "constantly, regularly, or habitually engaged in earnest and energetic work.[17] I don't think there is a description that fits gymnastics better. The entire sport consists of putting in your best effort for an extended period of time (having endurance) in order to succeed. By competing and training, you overcome so many obstacles that most people never have to endure. This builds your capacity for hard work, which you can apply in other areas of your life as well.

For me, I knew I had to work harder than most of my teammates because I wasn't necessarily as talented. But I had the drive to win. This meant putting in extra time, staying focused, and persisting despite difficulties. It also meant less talk and more action. It meant working hard when no one was watching so I could succeed when people were watching.

This relates to outside the gym as well. There may be others who are smarter or more gifted, but your gymnastics background teaches you the ability to outwork your competition. You understand the need to put in time, overcome obstacles, and persevere to be successful. This is a unique trait that will help you through all sorts of situations.

FACING FAILURE

Gymnastics is a master teacher of how to fail. More important, it is a master teacher of how to overcome failure. As a gymnast, you deal with so much failure that after a while it doesn't seem so scary. Many people avoid challenges because they are so afraid to fail—but not you. You know that when you fail you are one step closer to success. You also know that failure is a normal (and helpful) part of life.

Dealing with failure also makes you more resilient and creates the mindset that you can overcome hardships. Facing and overcoming failure is invaluable to growth and improvement. Even when something doesn't work out the first, second—or even sixth—time, you know how to keep persevering, working, and improving to eventually succeed.

Dealing with failure also includes having the right mindset. You've learned to have a positive attitude, even when things aren't going your way. You will fail, fall, or be afraid. This could ruin your day or the competition. Or you could choose to have a growth mindset and stay positive to overcome any adversity.

TEAMWORK

Gymnastics is interesting in that it is both an individual and a team sport. There are benefits to doing either individual or team sports, but you get the double benefit of a combination of the two! Research has found that those who participate in individual sports have greater conscientiousness and autonomy, while those who participate in team sports rank higher in agreeableness and interpersonal relationships.[18]

Although you compete as an individual, training long enough to get to that point is certainly a team effort. Teamwork is incorporated throughout practice by way of team conditioning, carrying mats together, cheering each other on, spotting one another, and generally being each other's support system. You also lean on teammates to help you overcome fears and help you through bad days. This collaborative environment fosters camaraderie and mutual trust, and it teaches the importance of cooperation.

Along with teamwork comes good sportsmanship: treating your teammates and competition with respect and support. This means being happy for your teammates if they do well, even if you didn't. Being positive and encouraging goes a long way.

ATTRIBUTES OF A HEALTHY TEAM

Teams are composed of different individuals but should always include these attributes to keep a healthy team environment:

- **Openness:** Members are open to other ideas, opinions, and viewpoints, without judgment.
- **Trust:** Team members trust each other and everyone is accountable.
- **Support:** Members help each other through challenging times to accomplish their individual and team goals.
- **Respect:** Team members are kind to each other, respect differences, and value each other.

HUMILITY

Being humble means you have confidence, but you also don't believe you are better than others. Gymnastics teaches humility because no matter how good you are, you still fail—constantly. Even when you have mastered a skill, you can still fall or land short, which keeps you humble.

What's interesting about gymnastics is that in some ways you have to be confident to be successful, but it's just as important to stay levelheaded and acknowledge that there are always new skills to learn and there is always room for improvement.

PATIENCE

Gymnastics is also a master teacher of patience. The first way gymnastics teaches patience is the basic lesson of waiting your turn. There are usually many gymnasts and only one coach. If you need a spot or want your coach to watch, then you need to have patience. This is taught at a very young age because lower levels typically have larger classes, and kids are particularly enthusiastic for their turn; however, they soon learn the need for patience. Their turn will come.

Then there is, of course, the patience required as you work to learn new skills and then even more patience as you work to perfect those skills. Practice is required when you try a skill again and again until it finally clicks. You have plenty of experience with delayed gratification—a situation when something takes longer than you expected—but the wait is certainly worth it. You understand the benefit of patience when you repeat a skill, make corrections, and try again and again.

Patience is also required to move up levels. When you're in level 5, you dream of conquering higher levels and the skills they require; however, you understand that you have to gradually work your way up to reach the higher levels. Even as you ascend the levels, your path may not always be a linear one (check out how I view progress in the next paragraph). For me, after level 8, I couldn't wait to be in level 9. But my coach thought it would be best for me to repeat level 8 before moving up. Although I was disappointed to be the only one in my group not moving up, I had to have patience and believe that this would benefit me in the long run. Sometimes you may even move up a level, try it, and then move back to the previous level. This is not moving backward; it is delayed gratification.

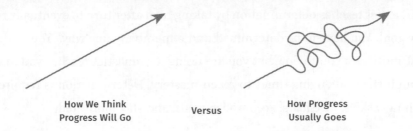

How We Think
Progress Will Go

Versus

How Progress
Usually Goes

Patience is also required if you get hurt. You must let your body heal, and then have patience again once you are cleared to return to practice if you are to avoid overstraining, reinjuring yourself, and further delaying your return.

Finally, every day you are practicing patience by returning to the skill or event that you have failed and failed again, until you finally succeed. You have the patience to continue to focus on your long-term goals, no matter the amount of time it takes to get there.

COURAGE

How many other sports require flipping on a four-inch beam, running into inanimate objects, or doing double backflips? Gymnastics is unique due to how often you are performing dangerous movements that could cause serious injury. What you do every day, most people could never even fathom doing!

It takes courage to learn new, difficult skills. Even after you've learned how to do the skill correctly, you may still experience fear. It takes courage to execute the skill or skills that scare you and trust your training, sometimes on a daily basis. There wasn't one day when I wasn't afraid to do my roundoff double-twist dismount on the beam, but I did it anyway because I knew I had proper training and would be safe. Gymnastics empowers you to conquer and overcome fears, which builds courage along the way.

DETERMINATION

Determination is persevering despite challenges and obstacles in order to reach your goals. Many skills in gymnastics are challenging and take time to master.

Gymnastics teaches determination by taking turn after turn to eventually reach your goal. You have to be determined and remember your "why." Your "why" is what motivates you to do what you are doing. Gymnastics teaches you to stick through the challenging times to reach mastery. Determination is required to learn new skills, face fears, accomplish goals, and stay motivated.

Write It Out

What is your "why"? What is your motivation to go to practice and train every day?

_____

_____

SMALL STEPS TO REACH BIG RESULTS

Gymnastics teaches you the need to take small steps in order to reach big results. For example, in order to do impressive level 10 or elite skills, you first have to learn how to do a handstand or forward roll. These skills may not feel impressive, but they are a necessary foundation. This is the premise of Stephen Duneier's TEDx Talk "How to Achieve Your Most Ambitious Goals."[19] Duneier says by breaking your large goals down into smaller and smaller pieces, you will be able to accomplish great feats. Through consistent determination, you build one skill onto the next, and then the next, mastering ever more difficult skills and then full routines. You can think of this idea like a book. First, focus on a single word. Then a full sentence, and then a single page, and then a chapter, until you have read an entire book and then an entire library of books! For Duneier, he used this technique to learn German. He listened to language tapes during his 45-minute walk to work. If you calculate 45 minutes of listening, twice a day, five days a week, for 52 weeks a year, then you can see how he used these small increments to eventually learn a whole new language. Trust in your determination that you can start small to reach your largest goals.

RESPECT

Gymnastics teaches many aspects of respect. The first is the respect of the athlete for other athletes. This means respecting your teammates, as well as your competitors. It includes cheering your teammates on and being gracious in both victory and defeat.

Respect learned in gymnastics also includes respect of the athlete for the coach. Something as simple as being on time to practice and greeting your coach every day when you walk in the gym shows respect. This is politeness but is also a form of respect. In my experience, at the beginning of practice every day, our coach would have us line up in order of height—with good posture required—and speak to us. Part of the respect was being attentive and listening to what he was saying. When your coach provides corrections, respect is also listening, looking them in the eye, acknowledging them, and making changes based on what they say. Following directions and responding appropriately and quickly to a critique enhances your gymnastics, helps avoid injury, and demonstrates respect.

There is also respect from coach to athlete. Even though your coach is critiquing and correcting you, they should also demonstrate respect for your thoughts and opinions. Your coach shows respect by believing in you and pushing you when they know you can do better. Mutual respect among all those associated with the team helps create a more positive and supportive team environment.

PERFORMING IN FRONT OF OTHERS WHILE UNDER PRESSURE

Being able to perform in front of others and perform under pressure is an often overlooked life lesson from gymnastics. You are constantly performing in front of others. This could be a practice competition where you present to your coach as if they were a judge and the rest of your team watches, or an actual competition with two to four judges watching you alongside an entire audience. Performing on demand and performing in front of others is no easy feat. When you participate in gymnastics, performing and being reviewed and judged simply become a part of your normal life. This skill translates into everything from public speaking, to performing on cue, to getting performance reviews at work. You have already performed for hundreds of people, doing much more challenging skills, so how hard could speaking in front of a few classmates be? When you've had multiple judges critiquing every little move you make, how hard could a job performance review be? Through your countless competitions and performances, you have learned how to work through nerves and be (or at least appear to be) calm and confident. Performing in front of peers and succeeding builds confidence (which we will dive into in chapter 5). All this is to say, you can handle pressure well, and in fact, are often at your best when performing under pressure, giving you the ability to succeed when others may wilt.

LEADERSHIP

Your leadership training in the gym starts at a young age. As you continue to grow in your gymnastics skills, your leadership skills also blossom. Gymnastics teaches you how to be a leader at any age, based on all the skills mentioned throughout this chapter. Your leadership skills are further strengthened as you get older, move up levels in gym, and are given more responsibility. For me, I began to feel like a true leader when I was in charge of leading the team warm-up. I also became a mentor to younger teammates and saw myself as a role model of hard work during practice. The leadership skills I learned through gymnastics translated into confidence, which led to me becoming a leader in other areas of life, from working on team assignments in school to taking on collaborative projects at work. The team-oriented mindset is instilled into every part of my life and continues to make me a better colleague, peer, and team member.

Gymnastics also teaches how to lead by example. By entering the gym every day, working hard, staying focused, showing dedication, and being supportive of others, you are being a great leader. Having the skill set of a leader, as well as experience in leadership positions, will make you a natural (even if informal) leader by inspiring others and taking ownership of the team's success.

You can probably think of life lessons, skills, and habits that I have missed. The life lessons and habits discussed in this chapter usually take time and often hardships or disappointment to learn; however, they will become a part of your identity and help you in all aspects of your life.

CHAPTER 3 KEY TAKEAWAYS

1. Gymnastics teaches countless life lessons that turn into positive habits. These life lessons make you a better gymnast and help you in other sports as well as the world outside gymnastics, whether it is school, work, or relationships.

2. These life lessons include time management, discipline, setting and achieving goals, commitment, facing failure, teamwork, humility, patience, courage, determination, respect, and performing in front of others while under pressure.

3. To be better at time management, avoid procrastinating, prioritize your tasks, set a schedule, make lists, and avoid multitasking. Finally, eat the frog! (Get the hardest or most important task out of the way first.)

4. Create SMART goals: specific, measurable, achievable, relevant, and time-based.

5. To achieve large, long-term goals, break them down into small, more manageable tasks. You will be amazed at what you can achieve.

CHAPTER 4

COORDINATION

Physical coordination is related to the physical benefits of gymnastics but is different enough to earn its own chapter.

Most sports require at least some level of coordination. Kicking a soccer ball requires you to run while simultaneously planning where to aim the ball. In baseball or softball, you need hand-eye coordination to be able to hit the ball flying toward you at just the right moment to hurl it into the outfield. These sports are impressive, but gymnastics takes coordination to a whole new level. Every skill requires you to be in control of your body and aware of what each limb is doing at every moment.

Because you've been training with this mind-muscle connection for so long, you may not even notice how aware you are of every muscle in your body; it's just what feels natural. This awareness has been drilled into your mind through the hours spent practicing and training the body and mind to do new tricks. Even the simplest skills require you to be highly aware of all your muscles and limbs. For example, a full turn seems simple, but while doing this turn, you are thinking about what your eyes are spotting on the wall, focusing on where your arms are in order to pull yourself around, holding your core tight and stomach in to maintain balance, and pushing on the ball of your foot while turning your heel to spin yourself around. If this is how much is going on in an uncomplicated turn, then just think about the thoughts, cues, and coordination required to do a Yurchenko or an Arabian!

WHAT IS PHYSICAL COORDINATION?

To start the discussion on building coordination, we should first talk about what coordination actually is. Coordination involves the senses as well as all parts of the body working together to move in a smooth or controlled way. Or, to put it more technically, it is the ability to coordinate muscle activation to produce smooth, efficient movements.[20] Coordination is certainly vital in sports to be able to move and react quickly and effectively.

When a coordinated person moves or plays a sport, that individual's movement looks effortless. An uncoordinated person, however, just can't seem to get everything working together—a leg doesn't move quickly enough or an arm doesn't strike in quite the correct way. The movement doesn't look easy or polished.

Although coordination is often thought of as purely genetic, training can significantly improve coordination.[21] In addition, coordination includes other components, such as balance, strength, and agility, which as we know from chapter 2, can all be improved with practice.

Training at a young age significantly improves coordination later in life. One study determined that between the ages of four and six is the crucial time for kids to hone their motor skills in order to be more agile, stronger, quicker, and more coordinated.[22] Coordination is a difficult skill to teach. Your best shot at being coordinated is to have proper development when you are young. By starting gymnastics at a young age, you are training your body and mind for better coordination, which is beneficial for your gymnastics, as well as any other sports you try.

COORDINATION TESTS

If you want to check how good your coordination is, then try a few of these tests.

1. Finger taps: Tap each finger on the thumb of one hand and then the other. See how fast you can make this movement.

2. Knee-to-shin slide: Sit down with your legs straight out in front of you. Touch your right heel to your left knee, and then run your heel down your shin until you reach your ankle. The smoother this movement is, the more coordinated you are.

3. Stick flip: Use two sticks to flip another stick. Try it five times. Give yourself one point for each successful half flip and two points for each full flip. How many points did you get?

4. Wall toss: Throw a ball against a wall using one hand and catching with the other. Try this for 30 seconds to see how many times you can catch the ball. Then try with the other arm.

5. Balloon taps: If you happen to have a balance board (or if there is one in your gym), then hop on and see if you can balance. You most likely are pretty good at that. To make it more challenging, grab a balloon and while balancing on the board, tap the balloon, switching off using your left and right hands to keep it in the air (right in front of you). See how long you can maintain your balance while keeping the balloon in front of you.

Two types of coordination are worth noting. Both are important to growth and development, and they allow you to perform different kinds of movements.

1. **Gross motor coordination:** This includes large muscles in the arms, legs, and torso for walking, running, lifting, and throwing.[23]
2. **Fine motor coordination:** This includes smaller muscles in the hands, wrists, and fingers, which allow writing, typing, brushing your teeth, and so on.[24]

Hand-eye coordination: Part of fine motor coordination is hand-eye coordination. This coordination involves sending information back and forth between what you're seeing and the muscles that need to move. It allows the body to react or do everyday tasks, such as cooking and using utensils, in addition to athletic endeavors, such as catching a ball, dribbling a ball, or jumping rope.

THE IMPORTANCE OF COORDINATION

We know that being coordinated allows you to move more easily, but it's important to note the benefits outside of sports performance. First, having better coordination is a great foundation to pick up any new exercise or activity. Your muscles and mind have already been trained, so when you learn something new, it is a smoother learning process. Along the same lines, coordination helps the body build muscle. Your muscle groups already know how to work together, so they can move cohesively to build strength or lift heavy things.

Having good coordination also aids in injury prevention for a few reasons: better balance, posture, and muscular control. Coordination allows you to move more efficiently and effectively, which means less strain, as well as wear and tear on joints and tissues. Coordination also helps prevent injuries because your body can respond better to sudden movements and changes in direction. This also relates to reacting quicker to stimuli. For example, if something is thrown at you, then you can react faster to quickly grab it or knock it away.

Additionally, coordination aids in muscle memory and in creating and maintaining neural connections in the brain. As you age, your body gets rid of the neural connections that it doesn't need. By continuing to train your body, particularly with coordination exercises, you are creating new connections to keep your mind healthy, active, and young.

COORDINATION VERSUS ATHLETICISM

Both coordination and athleticism are influenced by genetics. That said, through training, mindset, and lifestyle, they can both improve. As you know from the growth mindset, the mind is able to grow, change, and improve, and so is the body! Anything you think you're not good at can most likely be improved upon with practice and repetition.

Now that we know that both coordination and athleticism can progress, let's talk about what athleticism is. James Breese is an author, athlete, and founder of Strength Matters, a blog, podcast, and fitness business. Breese defines athleticism as a combination of ten physical qualities and characteristics: physical strength, agility, endurance (aerobic and anaerobic capacity), speed, power, mobility, stability, balance, and coordination.[25] There are also mental aspects of athleticism, including attitude, grit, competitiveness, and being able to perform under pressure.

Breese groups the qualities that make up athleticism into three layers. The base layer is the foundation for the second and third layers. Check out the performance pyramid:

STRENGTH MATTERS PERFORMANCE PYRAMID

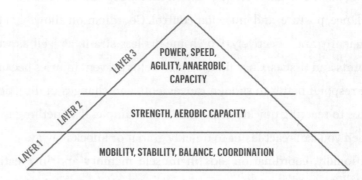

As you can see, coordination is part of the foundation for the other components of athleticism. Having good mobility, stability, balance, and coordination also decreases your likelihood of injuries, which aids in your pursuit of peak athleticism in the third layer.

Layer two is a continuation of the foundation that is layer one. If you have strength and aerobic capacity, then you will be successful in layer three. But if you don't have a good foundation in layers one and two, then you will be less likely to reach peak performance.

HOW GYMNASTICS HELPS WITH COORDINATION

Although good coordination helps you be successful in gymnastics, doing gymnastics also increases your coordination and body awareness through your skills, strength, and balance training. Gymnastics relies on the use of both gross and fine motor skills, as well as spatial awareness. Let's look at a few of the ways gymnastics improves your coordination.

CONSISTENCY

Through your consistent training, you are teaching the muscles how to work together and teaching the brain what neural connections to maintain and grow. Because there are always new skills to learn or new ways to think about your gymnastics, you are constantly sharpening your coordination skills.

BALANCE

Another way gymnastics helps build coordination is through balance training, which of course is a huge part of gymnastics. For example, on the beam the basic warm-up consists of walking on your toes, walking backward, hopping, and running—all on four inches of wood. This helps train balance and increase coordination.

Balancing on the beam is similar to strength training in that your muscles all have to be tight and work together to avoid falling off. Additionally, balance training keeps you aware (whether consciously or subconsciously) of where different body parts are so that you can stay on the beam. If half of your body is leaning one way and you don't bring it back to center, then you will surely fall.

Practicing on the balance beam also tests your reflex skills because if during a skill you start to go crooked, then your reflexes have to be sharp enough to compensate and keep you on the beam. Think about doing back walkovers or back handsprings on the beam: your body and mind are intently focused on being equal and aligned in order to stay in line with the four-inch beam. If an arm or a leg gets out of the correct plane, then it will throw you off. This training makes you cognizant of where your body is in space, thus improving coordination.

DANCE

A good portion of the floor for women's gymnastics requires dance, another great way to improve coordination. Dancing involves the entire body and all different muscle groups working together to move in a smooth, planned sequence. Sounds a lot like coordination, doesn't it?

Dance comes naturally for some, but for others (myself included) it can be a challenge. What is great about compulsory floor routines is that they are choreographed with fairly standard movements, which can help develop your dancing skills. Once you get your own floor routine, your choreographer will (with any luck) accommodate your dance skill level and make a floor routine that fits you. As your dance skills, confidence, and coordination improve, you can get a new floor routine that matches your enhanced dancing skills.

I had my strengths in gymnastics; however, dancing was never one of them. If you're like me, then you probably get a lot of flak for this from coaches or teammates. There are two ways to deal with this: either get a floor routine that doesn't require graceful dancing and just have sharp, strict movements, or work on your dance skills! You may be wondering when you'd have time to practice your dance skills on top of your training schedule, but dance does not have to take hours upon hours. Simply spending 10 minutes dancing in front of a mirror to see what looks good and what doesn't can dramatically improve your routine.

I had a teammate in college who had the most fun floor routine I'd ever seen. The music was upbeat, she had fantastic tumbling skills, and her dancing was contagious. When I asked her about her impeccable dance skills, she revealed that she hadn't always been a good dancer, but had slowly trained herself in front of a mirror. The end result was an entertaining, energetic routine that made everyone want to get out on the floor and start dancing too. Of course, her confidence made it even more of a showstopper, but her mirror practice really paid off.

Dancing uses the mind-body connection to move your body how you want it to. When training your floor routine, and particularly with choreography, there is a great deal of emphasis on what your arms, legs, head, fingers, and so on, are doing to make sure the movement looks good. Having the awareness of all the muscle groups and limbs to make them work together and in sync is all linked to improved coordination.

PROPRIOCEPTION

Along with increasing coordination, gymnastics is beneficial in developing proprioception, which is your brain's awareness of where your limbs are at any given moment. For example, if you hold out your arm, without actually seeing your hand, then you know whether your hand is flat and open, in a fist, or extending a certain number of fingers. This is because you can feel the energy exerted by your muscles in these various positions.

With better proprioception—awareness of our limbs and muscles—it is easier to make refinements to our movements. You can probably see where I'm going with this: being able to refine movement is essential for gymnastics. For example, proprioception helps when you are learning your back handspring on the beam. You need to push off with your legs, arch your back as you flip, and prepare your arms for your bodyweight before you push off to return to your feet. The more back handsprings you do, the less you have to think about what every muscle and limb is doing. Once you have that basic understanding, the next thing to focus on is refining the skill, or "cleaning up" the skill, as we'd say in gym. Your body has the basic understanding, but now you can focus on straightening your legs and pointing your toes. Having good proprioception allows you to move from "How do I do this?" to "How do I perfect this?"

Not only does proprioception help refine skills, but also it helps reduce the risk of injury and minimize muscle compensation. When you have better awareness of where your arms, legs, and head are, you are more likely to protect whatever needs protection when falling and less likely to overstrain your body.

IMPROVING COORDINATION OUTSIDE THE GYM

Certain exercises, drills, and activities benefit coordination by increasing balance, agility, and spatial awareness. The more you work on these activities, the better your coordination will become. Try some or all of the following:

- Tossing and catching a ball
- Jumping rope
- Walking lunges (also helps with balance and stability)
- Target exercises (aiming at a target, such as playing darts)
- Using your opposite hand (try brushing your teeth or brushing your hair with your nondominant hand)
- Skipping
- Jumping and landing on one foot
- Ladder drills
- Single-leg deadlift
- Jumping jacks
- Hopscotch
- Yoga
- Juggling (if you are feeling especially coordinated)

Although all these exercises are great ways to continue to improve your coordination, trying any new activity is also a fantastic way to build coordination. Your brain has to create new movement patterns for your muscles, which is beneficial for both the mind and body. In gymnastics, you are constantly learning new skills, which forces your brain to create new connections, which continue to improve your coordination.

In addition to the activities mentioned, getting a good night's sleep has a significant effect on coordination. Less sleep means less control of your body. When you think about a chronic lack of sleep, you can see how it wears down coordination over time.

Stress can also affect coordination. Mentally, when we feel stressed, the brain processes more slowly and our reaction time decreases. Physically, stress causes our muscles to tense so movements aren't so smooth (also making injuries more likely).[26]

So in addition to training, the many activities previously listed, as well as learning new activities, getting enough sleep and avoiding stress are additional ways outside gymnastics to improve coordination.

MIND-BODY CONNECTION

You may have heard of the mind-body connection and how your mental state affects your physical body or how the state of your body determines your mindset. For example, when you feel mentally stressed, your heart rate and blood pressure automatically increase. Conversely, breathing exercises bring down your heart rate and blood pressure, and eventually also calm the mind.

The mind-body connection and coordination are intertwined. Having good coordination means that your muscles are all working together harmoniously. This involves the brain telling different muscle groups to move. Then these muscles must work together cohesively to do the correct movements, following your brain's instructions. This is where the power of visualization comes in. You can have an image or movement in your head, but if you don't have the mind-body connection to make your muscles move how your brain wishes, then it will never turn out as planned.

In college gymnastics, before competitions, our coach would have us visualize what a successful routine looked like for each event. We visualized success from the moment we saluted to the judge to the final landing. Our coach knew that the first step to success was envisioning what would happen, which would connect the mind and body to coordinate the movements before they happened. By prepping both the body and mind, our muscles were already conditioned and coordinated. All they had to do was follow the movements that we had been training, both mentally and physically.

THE BENEFITS OF VISUALIZATION

Michael Phelps, Olympic swimmer and the most decorated Olympian of all time, is a huge proponent of visualization.

He started using visualization at thirteen to mentally prepare for his races. Phelps explained that he would start mentally preparing a month before a large meet to visualize what *could* happen, what he *wanted* to happen, and what *could* go wrong. This way, whatever happened, he was prepared for it.[27] Visualizations can be you watching yourself compete (as someone in the stands) or competing as you would see it through your own eyes. Visualizations also need to be vivid and rehearsed again and again. Phelps explains that the countless visualizations and mental rehearsals allowed him to go on autopilot as soon as he walked into a race.

Another example of the mind-body connection is a conditioning technique I learned in club gymnastics: the mind-muscle connection. During conditioning, think about and touch the exact muscle or muscles you are strengthening. For example, during side crunches, place your hand on your side ab to connect your brain to the muscle that is being worked. When you touch your muscle, this helps form a tactile feedback loop between your brain and whatever muscle you are working, which helps activate that muscle and make it stronger. Check out the photos that follow for reference.

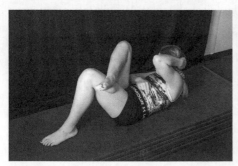 

These two different ab movements demonstrate the athlete touching the exact core muscle that she is working in order to better strengthen it.

Some studies show that if you use mental imagery and visualize yourself doing skills while injured, then you come back from that injury more easily.[28] You might be skeptical but it makes sense! There are multiple reasons that visualization, and in particular positive visual imagery, helps with the recovery process:

1. Visualizing themselves performing the skills motivates athletes to return to their sport.
2. It also allows athletes to retain vivid mental images of recent performance, which can aid in the retention of motor skills.[29]
3. Visualization also enhances the coping skills of injured athletes.
4. It allows athletes to more readily adhere to a rehabilitation regime.
5. Visualizing or rehearsing movements helps injured athletes maintain their fundamental skills.

As Marty Durden, EdD, says in his article "Utilizing Imagery to Enhance Injury Rehabilitation," "If an athlete can first see it, then she can do it—this is the essence of visualization."[30] The mind and body are incredibly intertwined, and this connection creates the coordination to accomplish extraordinary tasks and success in gymnastics.

CHAPTER 4 KEY TAKEAWAYS

1. Coordination is the ability to get various body parts to work together in a smooth or controlled way.
2. Athleticism is made up of ten qualities, with coordination being part of the foundation of athletic achievement.
3. Gymnastics is beneficial for coordination because it offers balance, strength, and agility training, all of which are important to coordination. In addition, most gymnasts start the sport at a young age, which helps them gain maximum benefit from that training.
4. Certain exercises require coordination and therefore increase coordination. These include catching a ball, jumping, skipping, and yoga.
5. The mind-body connection is essential for coordination, to compete well, to get stronger, and to come back from injuries quicker.

CHAPTER 5

CONFIDENCE

"Your success will be determined by your own confidence and fortitude."

—Michelle Obama

Let's switch gears and discuss how gymnastics builds confidence. We will dive in with the definition of confidence, continue with a discussion of what confidence is versus what it is not, and then discuss ways to continue to build and maintain confidence.

Particularly with kids, exercising and competing in sports are common prescriptions for building confidence. There are a few reasons for this, with the first being the fact that exercise and sports make you move! Moving causes the body to release natural feel-good hormones called endorphins. Exercising also makes you feel accomplished, reduces stress, and leads to a better body self-image. Sports are usually social activities, which help to build friendships and deep bonds.

Although these points are worth noting, I've also often found confidence to be paradoxical in gymnastics. In many ways, gymnastics bruises your confidence by constantly telling you that you're not good enough and need to be better at X, Y, and Z skills. But in other ways, it is a foundation for confidence based on the reasons just discussed, as well as the fact that it makes you stronger, fitter, more coordinated, and highly skilled at an incredibly challenging sport. In many ways, gymnastics breaks down your confidence and then builds it back up even stronger.

WHAT IS CONFIDENCE?

It's important to first understand what confidence is and what it feels like to be confident. Confidence is believing that you can meet challenges and overcome obstacles, even things that scare you![31] Another way to think about confidence is having conviction in your abilities, which can be backed by evidence. For example, when you first started gymnastics, you had a lot to learn. You probably weren't winning any competitions, and you weren't telling anyone that you were a star athlete. But as your skills improved and training progressed, you may have started placing or even winning competitions. This probably made you realize that, "Hey, I'm actually good at this." And slowly your confidence in your gymnastics abilities began to grow.

Have you ever met someone that you were immediately drawn to for some reason? Oftentimes, we are drawn to their confidence. Confident people come across as more likable and credible, and they seem to be better at dealing with pressure as well as facing and overcoming challenges. When you're around a confident person, sometimes their self-assuredness can also make you feel better about yourself. For all these reasons, research has shown that confident people are more likely to be elevated to positions of status and leadership.[32]

Going back to the growth mindset, being confident means you trust in your abilities, but still understand that you make mistakes, experience weaknesses, and have areas of improvement. Your confidence grows when you recognize that you are good at something. At the same time, gymnastics makes sure you aren't too confident because you are constantly falling, failing, and working to get better. What a perfect combination! You should believe that you are a good gymnast and athlete while at the same time knowing that you can always improve.

CONFIDENCE AND LEADERSHIP

Why are we so sure that confident people are great leaders? Well, we see this correlation often, and although confidence does not necessarily mean you are a great leader, confident athletes and candidates are more likely to win and confident businesspeople are more likely to succeed.[33] Even if confidence doesn't actually make you a better leader, confident people tend to be more open to critique, are better at decision-making, are seen as more trustworthy, and are more likely to empower others on their team—all characteristics of a good leader.

WHAT CONFIDENCE IS NOT

Now that we know what confidence is, it's important to talk about what it is not. Confidence is not being the loudest person in the room. It is not being arrogant or a know-it-all. Sometimes confidence can come across as arrogance and arrogance can come across as confidence, but there are serious differences. Confidence is believing in your abilities because you have evidence of your success. Arrogance, on the other hand, is overestimating or exaggerating your abilities, without proof to back up your claims. Also, having confidence means that you want and believe that you can (and should) work to keep improving. Sounds a lot like the growth mindset, doesn't it? Arrogant people think they don't need to change, which demonstrates a fixed mindset. In addition, they put others down or highlight others' flaws to feel better about themselves.

THE COMFORT ZONE

Something else that confidence is *not* is living in your comfort zone. Your comfort zone is where you feel safe, and where your ability and determination are not tested.[34] This sounds like the opposite of confidence, doesn't it? Confidence is where you are testing your ability and pushing yourself. In your comfort zone, there is no need to push yourself. You feel safe and that's a great feeling. If something is difficult or really pushes you, then you probably feel as if you want to quit, because that's easier. I know this feeling! I went through a period of months when I belly flopped my Gienger every day on the bars. I often thought how much better it would be if I simply stopped doing this release move, or if I stopped training on the bars altogether. But that would have been the easy way out. Avoiding this skill wasn't pushing my abilities or determination. And the

Gienger became a bigger and bigger obstacle the more I avoided it. I had to step out of my comfort zone, try my release move in a different way, and figure out the root cause of why I was missing it.

If you stay in your comfort zone and don't force yourself to think or act any differently, then you will begin to doubt yourself and lose confidence in yourself. Once you can push out of the comfort zone, you are forced to grow. You will see that you are in fact capable of that skill and you will have more confidence for trying it. Once you step out and see what can come from pushing yourself, you are more likely to get outside your comfort zone again.

EXCUSES

Another thing that confidence is *not* is making excuses. Making excuses is creating reasons why you cannot do something, while confidence is proving to yourself that you can. When you create excuses and avoid, you are not letting yourself test your abilities. Avoidance keeps you exactly where you are. Making excuses becomes a habitual response and causes the vicious excuse cycle that follows:

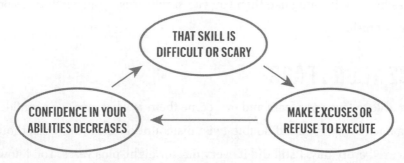

Let's break it down: when you refuse to do that difficult or scary thing, your confidence in yourself, the thing that makes you say, "I can do this," decreases. This means that the next time you're faced with a challenge, you won't have the confidence to go for it, which decreases your confidence even more. You have now created a list (which will continue growing) of things you can't do because you've never tried. By getting rid of excuses and getting out of your comfort zone, you will see that confidence is just on the other side.

BUILDING CONFIDENCE

Now that we understand what confidence is and is not, how exactly do we build confidence? Confidence grows by trying, maybe failing, but eventually (with any luck) achieving. Pushing yourself through something difficult and then over-coming it is a great way to build confidence. Sounds like a regular day in the gym, doesn't it?

Once you try that difficult skill, it can either go well or poorly, but you still gave it a shot! This is an accomplishment and you feel good about yourself for trying. This builds your confidence that you can do difficult things and it will be okay. Then, the next time you're faced with a difficult skill, you have the confidence to go for it.

Think about the skills you have. You swing around bars, flip on four inches, and do double flips and twists. Just look at all the things you accomplish on a daily basis compared with what "normal" people do. That in itself should give you a confidence boost. Gymnastics also puts daunting tasks into perspective. For example, if you can learn your new bar dismount or make it through that impossible conditioning list, then you can surely crush your math test—or ask out your crush.

FACE YOUR FEARS

Being able to face your fears and overcome them is what gives you confidence. Going back to my roundoff double-twist dismount on the beam, even though I was scared every day, I still did it every day for eight-plus years. You know the saying, "Do one thing every day that scares you?" Well, how many people actually do that? I know I did and I'm sure you do too. Whether it's on the beam or another event, having that achievement of facing and overcoming your fears is a great way to demonstrate belief in yourself.

ACHIEVEMENTS

Knowing that you are good at something builds your confidence. You are training day in and day out. You can see progress in your routines and increases in your scores. Seeing your growth builds confidence, and understanding that you can overcome and succeed despite obstacles is essential for confidence.

THE KITCHEN SINK

Have you ever heard someone talking about throwing in "everything but the kitchen sink"? Well, that phrase means including everything possible, and I'm about to throw in every reason possible for you to have confidence in yourself:

Confidence in athleticism: Because of your training, you are strong and flexible and you have good balance, coordination, and endurance, all of which make you a better all-around athlete. This wins you more confidence in conquering gymnastics and any other sport.

Confidence in fitness: Along with feeling good, your training gives you a fit, toned body. Knowing that you are fitter and healthier than the average person is another way to boost your confidence.

Confidence through positivity: Playing sports and being physically active improves your quality of sleep. As you know, each day as a gymnast is long and exhausting. This means that you fall asleep faster and have deeper sleep. Better sleep means a better mood and mental outlook for the next day (also known as more positivity).

Confidence in academic success: Better sleep also means better concentration, critical thinking skills, learning ability, and judgment. All these factors make you a better student and more confident in your academic abilities.

Confidence in leadership ability: Practicing your leadership skills in the gym through mentoring, leading warm-up, or being a role model means that people look up to you, which builds your confidence as a leader. Your leadership skills translate outside the gym as well.

LOOK GOOD, FEEL GOOD, DO GOOD

Wait, there's more! In addition to the many ways to develop confidence already listed, something else that was drilled into my head in gym was good posture. My coach believed that there were many reasons why good posture was essential in the gym. Holding yourself with good posture made you *look* more confident but could also translate into *feeling* more confident. Good posture meant holding the shoulders back, with the head high and the hands on the hips. We were never allowed to hug ourselves. Not only do you look less confident when you hug yourself, but also your shoulders naturally hunch, making you look and feel weaker. Always remember: look good, feel good, do good. Can you see the difference in the pictures that follow? Try it out for yourself!

These photos demonstrate how the difference in the way you hold yourself and present yourself to the world affects your confidence. When you stand like the left photo, with your chest and chin up and with your hands on your hips, you look and feel more confident.

On the right, this bad posture makes you look and feel less confident. See how her shoulders are rounded and her arms hug herself. Feel the difference between these two images in yourself.

Confident posture   Bad posture

Write It Out

Write down how both your body and mind feel different when you have good and bad posture.

Example: "When I hunch my shoulders, I look and feel small and weak. When I hold my shoulders back and head high, I feel powerful and unstoppable."

_____

_____

Along the same lines as "Look good, feel good, do good," I remember the confidence I felt when putting on my shiny leotard, braiding my hair, and adding sparkles everywhere. It felt special to put on my competition leotard and do my hair for 30 minutes (sometimes more). So in addition to how I physically held myself, making myself feel good about my appearance helped create a feeling of confidence that turned into real confidence. When you feel more confident, you perform better. Create that for yourself.

FAKE IT TILL YOU MAKE IT

You may have heard the saying "Fake it till you make it." A variant of this saying is "Fake it till you feel it." Even when you are not feeling confident, you can fake confidence until it becomes real. By holding yourself with good posture—shoulders back and head high—you are appearing confident, which can actually convince your brain that you are confident.

STRIKE A POWER POSE

One technique I learned to feel more confident and powerful is a power pose. It is essentially taking up more space with your body. By standing with your shoulders back, your feet in a wide stance, and your arms either showing off your muscles (photos 1 and 2 on page 84), hands on your hips (photo 3), or even hands behind your head, or in the air in a *Y*, you look more powerful and as a result you feel more powerful. This is the opposite of how you look and feel when you hug yourself and hunch over.

When your mind feels powerful (maybe you've just won a race), the automatic physical response is to raise your hands in the air in celebration. Your body follows how your mind feels. But it can work in the opposite direction as well. When you strike a power pose with your body, you look confident and this can convince your mind of that confidence as well.

So the next time you're feeling down at practice or in a competition, strike a power pose. Hold it for 15 to 30 seconds, and you will notice a significant difference in your mental state.

Photo 1   Photo 2   Photo 3

SETTING AND ACHIEVING YOUR GOALS

Another way gymnastics builds your confidence is through you setting and achieving goals. As we talked about previously, a lot of gymnastics is centered around setting SMART goals and then working to achieve them. Once you achieve a goal that you have set (either a short-term, medium-term, or long-term goal), it is another boost to your confidence. You are demonstrating that by working hard, you are able to achieve what you wanted—and that is a great feeling. You are accomplishing tasks (difficult skills in this case), which means you feel able to accomplish more and more in the future, and the confidence cycle continues.

AFFIRMATIONS

Finally, even when you are implementing all the tricks and methods already mentioned, sometimes you will still need to remind yourself of how great you truly are. Affirmations are statements that you tell yourself when you feel down or uncertain. These can be statements such as, "I am capable" or "I am confident in my abilities." At first it may feel silly to look into a mirror and talk to yourself, but give it a shot. It may be the very boost you need for your confidence.

ASK THE EXPERT: CASSIE RICE

As you can see, there are many ways to build confidence on your own; however, your coach can also be a great resource. Here's what coach Cassie Rice, founder and owner of GymCats (in Henderson, Nevada) has to say:

"Coaches can help athletes build confidence by allowing them to dictate how fast or slow they move through levels and add skills. If an athlete feels they are pushed too fast and then crash, this will destroy their confidence and [they will] lose their trust in the entire process. The moving slowly part is really important to keep building confidence, especially as they get to higher level skills."

"Coaches also need to make sure they have a really open line of communication, so the athlete can be free to communicate whatever they're feeling, no matter what that is, and that will build trust and confidence as well. If a coach creates a culture that is to 'shut up and do as you're told,' then athletes will be very fearful and less likely to attempt new things."

THE BENEFITS

Now that we know what confidence is and how to build it, let's look at the actual benefits of self-confidence.

INCREASED SUCCESS

Saying that confidence increases success is a broad statement, but greater confidence means you believe that you can accomplish your goals. Even when you have setbacks, because of your confidence you will continue to work to reach that success. Someone without confidence is more likely to give up before they achieve success.

The quote from Michelle Obama at the beginning of this chapter perfectly demonstrates how success is fully in your own hands. Success relies on your self-confidence and fortitude (or grit); once you have these two things, the sky is the limit.

LESS FEAR AND ANXIETY

Greater self-confidence means you are willing to take more risks and venture outside your comfort zone. You know that even when something doesn't work the first time, you have confidence in your abilities to keep working and eventually get there. Self-confidence also helps quiet your inner critic. Additionally, greater confidence means that you are not ruminating about every worry or mistake.

GREATER RESILIENCE

Having greater confidence means you have the skills and coping methods to handle setbacks. It also means that you can recover quicker from setbacks. You understand that setbacks are normal, even helpful, in your pursuit of excellence. If you have confidence, then a failure or something going wrong won't ruin you. You are resilient, able to bounce back.

Confident people are also better at handling criticism. They understand that constructive criticism is meant to help them improve and is just another step on their path. Being able to face, accept, and respond to criticism is useful for gaining a new perspective.

BETTER RELATIONSHIPS

Having confidence is also beneficial for your friendships and relationships. With confidence comes the ability to state your boundaries, assert your needs, be open with people, and communicate effectively. This allows you to connect with people more easily, as well as build better, more meaningful relationships.

When you are confident in yourself, you are able to interact with others more authentically. You believe people like you for yourself, and there is no need to act like someone you are not.

HEALTHIER LIFESTYLE

Confidence, particularly the confidence that comes from sports, makes you want to keep getting stronger, fitter, and better. You continue to live a healthy lifestyle because it will make you a better athlete. People with low self-confidence, on the other hand, don't have the same motivation for a healthy lifestyle. They are more likely to engage in risky or unhealthy behaviors, such as drinking, drugs, or smoking,[35] all of which have negative health consequences.

HAPPINESS

For all the reasons stated and more, confident people tend to be happier.[36] Confident people have greater success, are more decisive, have less fear and anxiety, experience greater resilience, enjoy better relationships and stronger connections, are better able to reach their goals, feel better about themselves, and have a generally more positive view of life. These are all great ways to enhance your happiness and outlook on life.

CONFIDENCE VERSUS SELF-ESTEEM

Confidence and self-esteem are often viewed as the same thing, but there are important differences. Confidence is how you project yourself to those around you. You can build confidence through having a specific skill set, such as gymnastics. Your confidence grows through practice and accomplishments that others see. Self-esteem, on the other hand, is how you see yourself on the inside. It is not related to the skills you possess.

You can become more confident by being good at something and being able to demonstrate your skills. Self-esteem is more like self-worth, which comes from how you view and talk to yourself and can be affected by family, society, and environment. This is why it's important to have both confidence and self-esteem! Your confidence can grow when you gain more skills (external validation), but self-esteem can grow only if you are conscious of your internal narrative: how you think about and talk to yourself.

WHAT TO DO WITH NEGATIVE THOUGHTS

Despite your training, improvements, accomplishments, good posture, and wins, you—like all human beings—have a nagging voice in your head saying that you are not good enough or that you can't succeed. This is your negative internal narrative, and it's difficult to build your confidence and self-esteem with that voice disparaging you. The National Science Foundation found that each of us has around 60,000 thoughts a day. Of these, around 80 percent are negative thoughts.[37] That's a lot of negative thoughts! Good thing you have ways to overcome this negative self-talk.

REFRAME

You have a choice to make when negative thoughts creep in. You can surrender to them, letting all your training and confidence go out the window. Or you can reframe your thoughts and create a different narrative. Check out the table on page 27 for examples of negative thoughts being reframed to positive thoughts.

From my personal experience with negative thoughts, I know that these voices are very loud and intrusive, and it's much easier said than done to turn them off. But as you know, the more you practice something, the easier it becomes. The more you practice changing and reframing negative thoughts to positive ones, the weaker and less impactful they will become.

REPLACE WITH POSITIVITY

In addition to reframing, use positive truths to turn off the negative self-talk. No matter what level or skill set you have, you have improved and continue to improve. Tell yourself that! There is at least one skill that you once couldn't do and now you can; that's an accomplishment. You used to always bend your legs but now you can keep them straight; that's an accomplishment. You used to be afraid of that back walkover, but now you can do it on the beam; that's an accomplishment. These are wins and don't you forget them! Our brains tend to focus more on the negatives, but you are able to switch back to the positives and think about all the things you have done so you can get back to a more positive and confident mindset.

You are in control of your own body. More important, you are in charge of your own mind. Your thoughts become reality, so as much as you can, stay on top of these negative thoughts to bring yourself back to a better, more confident place.

WINNER'S MINDSET

After shifting from negative thoughts to positive ones, how do we maintain positive thoughts to create a winner's mindset? This is a state of mind that focuses on achieving success through self-confidence, motivation, resilience, and mental toughness.[38]

As you can see, one of the best ways to create a winner's mindset is to have confidence in yourself, to know that you can accomplish what you want to accomplish. A winner's mindset relies on a growth mindset, which you can continue to improve through your efforts. Finally, as we talked about in chapter 1, grit—the ability to persevere through challenges—is a large part of the winner's mindset.

Focus on what has gone right instead of what hasn't. Start with the small wins. Maybe it's getting yourself to the gym that day. From there, you made it through the warm-up and are feeling good. Next, you excelled in conditioning. Or perhaps it was a different small win. Focus on those! From there, the big wins will come. For a week or two, just focus on the small wins and see if your mindset changes.

Your training in the gym makes you a better, more confident gymnast and person. You will be tested many times in your life. As long as you hold a core belief in yourself, you will be able to get through any obstacle. Having trust and confidence in yourself makes you unstoppable. Start with the affirmation "I believe in myself," and see where that takes you. You've got this!

CHAPTER 5 KEY TAKEAWAYS

1. Confidence is having the belief that you can meet challenges and overcome obstacles.

2. Confidence is getting out of your comfort zone and not making excuses.

3. Build your confidence by facing your fears, setting and achieving goals, mastering skills, and stating positive affirmations.

4. Confidence makes you more successful in the gym, at school, and at work; reduces stress and anxiety; creates resilience, better relationships, and a healthier lifestyle; and boosts your overall happiness.

5. When negative thoughts creep in, reframe them and focus on the positives to create and maintain a winner's mindset.

THE SOCIAL SIDE

"Friendships born on the field of athletic strife are the real gold of competition. Awards become corroded; friends gather no dust."

—Jesse Owens,
US track and field Olympian

Outside the physical and mental advantages, coordination, and self-confidence that gymnastics fosters, one of its most important benefits is the deep bonds created, developed, and nurtured during training. An important appeal of the sport and reason why we keep coming back, despite the bad days and downsides, is the opportunity to build and strengthen social connections every day in the gym. Gymnastics can also build strong, meaningful connections with mentors and coaches who push you to your full potential in and out of the gym.

GYM FRIENDS

Maybe you started gymnastics with a friend or joined to make friends. Either way, you now spend countless hours each day with your teammates. You are bound to get to know each other and connect over the sport, at the very least.

There is something about going through the unique experience of practicing for hours every day that builds deep friendships. Together with your teammates, you face good days and bad days, learn new skills, sweat, cry, lean on each other, and fiercely compete both with and against each other. It's hard to think of a better bonding experience, especially at such a young age.

Having teammates who are going through or have gone through the same difficulties as you also builds kinship. You probably have a teammate who has been through a similar experience with an injury, fear, or frustration, who can empathize, let you vent, or share coping strategies.

Even traveling to competitions when you drive, fly, or stay in hotels together gives you unique memories that you will most likely never experience with friends outside gymnastics.

There is also something to be said for constantly being surrounded by people who have the same mindset as you. In one sense, you are the same type of crazy for being willing to practice 25-plus hours a week, but you also have the same disciplined, determined, and courageous mindset. Because of your training, you have a bounce-back mindset instilled in you. Being around people who think the same way as you encourages this healthy mindset and further connects you.

You may have heard the saying "You are the average of the five people you spend the most time with." Well, you'd probably love to be a combination of your teammates: focused, persistent, dedicated, hardworking, and brave.

Aside from the same training regimen and mindset, you most likely even have a similar body type as your teammates. There is something comforting about being around people who are just as muscular as you are, particularly at this age. I always stood out in school because of my broad shoulders and strong legs. Although muscles are certainly a good thing, when you're the only muscular girl, it can feel isolating. Your teammates know what it's like to be incredibly strong and fit at such a young age. At the gym you fit right in.

These are just a few examples of how everyday interactions that seem small can add up to become meaningful connections and lifelong friendships.

Write It Out

Write down your favorite part of having gym friends. How do gym friends help you get through gym, school, and life in general?

_____

_____

THE BENEFITS

There are countless benefits to creating friendships at a young age and through sports. Strong friendships in childhood and adolescence are particularly beneficial for developing social and emotional skills, as well as increasing a sense of belonging. Children with strong friendships have "higher self-esteem, act more socially, can cope with life stresses and transitions, and are also less victimized by peers."[39]

In adolescence, meaningful friendships are not only important for greater self-esteem and lower rates of anxiety, depression, and stress, but also are important to feel understood, to experience being supported, and to help build a burgeoning identity.[40]

BELONGING

Being part of a team gives you a sense of belonging; you are part of something. It also means that others rely on you. Your teammates may count on your solid routines or good scores to contribute to the team score. Your role could also be that you are a great pre-meet pep talker, motivator, or mat mover; whatever your role is, you are an essential part of the team and add value.

Gymnastics also creates a sense of belonging because when you are at a meet, you and your teammates are all wearing the same shiny leotard, so it is clear who your team—your tribe, your people—are. It is the same when traveling to competitions together.

REAL CONNECTION

We live in an online world. Although there are certain benefits to being able to connect virtually, we often lack real connection, making us lonelier than older generations despite our interconnectedness. Another benefit of being in the gym is spending time together each day, face-to-face and offline. Most days in school or at home are spent looking at screens in one form or another, either computers, televisions, cell phones, or smart boards. In the gym, however, you have to be fully present without hiding behind any screens.

Although it is possible to build friendships online, practicing together in person is a much quicker way to build trust and connection. Going through the ups and downs of a sport together, your teammates see your good, bad, and ugly sides, while with online connections, you might share only your best self.

SOCIAL SKILLS

Significant social skills are developed through gymnastics that lead to lasting friendships and make you a better friend overall. Let's check them out.

Teamwork and Selflessness

One of the most basic aspects of being in a gym is moving mats around. It's a team effort to move a large mat from one side of the gym to the other. Team members must cooperate and coordinate to lift the giant mat over their heads, communicate any obstacles along the way, and safely place the mat down without it landing on anyone. This is one of the first ways that teamwork is learned in the gym.

Because gymnastics is both an individual and a team sport, in a competition setting you have to be focused and prepare for your own performance while also being an encouraging teammate, cheering others on and celebrating their victories. Selflessness goes beyond clapping for your teammates; it also means sharing turns, equipment, and hair spray, as well as moving boards, mats, and bar settings.

Learning how to listen, support friends, and be selfless in the gym teaches you how to be a better friend outside the gym as well. Selfless people are those who are genuinely kind, caring, thoughtful, and understanding, with no strings attached. Being a selfless friend also helps you attract other selfless friends.

Trust

Another aspect of being part of a team is relying on each other and having trust in each other. You have to trust that your teammates will do their job (execute their routines to help the team score), just as you will do your job for the benefit of the team.

When there is trust on a team, the team becomes stronger, more effective, and more cohesive. Putting trust in someone else and having them trust you creates a bond and a feeling of closeness. Being able to trust others helps the team succeed. Trusting others also helps you be a good friend.

HOW TO BUILD TRUST

To succeed as a team, you need to be able to trust your teammates and for them to trust you. What can you do right now to start building that trust? Here are a few ideas:

1. Communicate openly: If you want others on your team to communicate openly and honestly, then start with yourself. Are you talking in a way that is honest, kind, and respectful? Be open to what's going on with you (your frustrations, fears, challenges, and successes), and see how your teammates also open up.

2. Be reliable and dependable: Being reliable and dependable means showing up on time and following through on things you say you will do. If your teammates know you are reliable and dependable, then they will follow suit.

3. Show empathy: When you show empathy for others, you demonstrate compassion and understanding. This automatically builds an emotional connection. When we are more connected, we are more trusting.

4. Acknowledge and learn from mistakes: Missteps—blunders, errors, mistakes—happen. If you take responsibility for your mistakes and work to learn from them, then you are showing that you are human. This also helps others be more trusting and allows them to learn and grow from your mistakes, as well as their own.

Cooperation

Being part of a team and being around other team members so much means that sometimes you will not agree with them. Even when you disagree, you and they are still teammates and have to cooperate to be around each other so many hours each day. Cooperation is a foundational skill of being a good friend, coworker, and colleague, and this skill will benefit you in school, on work projects, and in life.

SCHOOL FRIENDS VERSUS GYM FRIENDS

Although school friendships are extremely important, there is no substitute for gym friends. Sports bring people from different locations, schools, and backgrounds together and allow you to be friends with people you might never have met otherwise.

Most of my closest friendships even years after being out of the sport were friends I met through club or college gymnastics. It is great to have school friendships, but those relationships are different. Those friends do not understand the time constraints that you face as a gymnast. They don't understand why you can't hang out every day after school or what that weird blister on your hand is.

For me, school could feel isolating for a multitude of reasons. I didn't take the bus to school. I slept in and my parents drove me to school because I got home from practice so late. Also, I left school an hour earlier than my peers (because I didn't take gym class), so I could make it to practice on time. In addition, I didn't do any extracurricular activities after school, such as theater or dance, because I was always at practice. Finally, I often couldn't attend school social outings, such as school dances or football games, due to my gym schedule. I didn't spend as much time with school friends and therefore didn't feel as close to them.

And my gym friends had very similar school experiences. We spent enough time in school to learn what we needed to and then headed straight for the gym.

Sometimes it felt more like school friends were friends while gym friends were more like family.

I also loved how gym friends didn't know anyone at my school. I could talk freely about my school crushes and anything else going on at school. There was something liberating about living two lives.

Additionally, middle school and high school can be an extremely challenging time. Many things are changing, and this can often include friends changing. When challenges or conflicts occur, friends who are separate from school can serve as a refuge and support system outside your school circle.

BONDING

Gymnastics bonds you with your teammates in countless ways. I'm sure you have many examples yourself. Following are a few examples of my own.

During practice my coach would say something like, "If Julia makes this skill or sticks the landing, then we can move on to the next event." Of course, this was to create pressure, but it also evoked a sense of loyalty and duty to my teammates. I felt pressure and nerves because I didn't want to let my teammates down. We were all tired and wanted to go to the next event. When you were in the hot seat, you tried your hardest to perform and not disappoint everyone. When you were watching your teammate and the task was out of your hands, you had to have complete faith in that person. This was a great way to practice for meets, but it also bonded us and made us rely on and trust each other.

Even partner conditioning is a bonding experience. Many conditioning exercises involve someone holding your legs or feet for sit-ups, other core exercises, or handstand holds. In a handstand hold, you have to communicate with your partner, as well as trust the other person to help you stay balanced. You are also keeping your partner accountable by calling out where they could be tighter or if they have bad form. As a partner, you are physically supporting them, but you are also making them a better gymnast by helping perfect their handstand, which is the foundation of many skills.

Another bonding experience was if we didn't finish our assignment during the allotted time in practice, at the end of practice we would have to go back to that event and complete the assignment. It was always arduous to return at the end of practice after working out for the past five hours, our hands sore and ripped, and having to do even more routines. Despite the challenge of added work after a long day of school and practice, it bonded us when we spent those extra 30 minutes to an hour trying to squeeze out that last routine. We got through this difficult experience together.

There was also the bonding time of gym sleepovers. Even after spending all those hours together in the gym, somehow we wanted to spend even more time together. We'd all go to someone's house and watch movies, play games, polish each other's nails, and stay up late. It never felt like we had enough time together. That's the type of friendship gymnastics encourages: you can't get enough of each other.

Even days when we'd clean the pit were team bonding memories. We would all be in our pit cleaning attire, which usually entailed a mask and gloves to prevent the tiny bits of pit from getting in our eyes and mouths. It wouldn't matter anyway. because we would always end up with tiny blue shreds of foam in our hair, on our skin, and tucked into our leotards. Then we would take on the daunting task of removing all the foam blocks, uncovering hair ties, adhesive bandages, clips, socks, coins, and on occasion a stray dollar bill. After vacuuming the bottom and putting in new blocks, the task was complete. The whole ordeal would take a few hours, but what I remember most are all the giggles and shrieks from what we would discover and the fact that we got to miss practice for a day. Although I would never volunteer to clean a gymnastics pit today, with all the sweat, pee, and who knows what else in it, those are cherished bonding memories.

College gymnastics was a whole new level of bonding. First, I lived with teammates all four years, which meant we had the shared experience of training in the gym every day together, but we also ate meals, commuted to school, and went to classes together. That is a lot of bonding time!

Training in college also meant preseason 5 a.m. cardio conditioning sessions. This was in addition to the regular practice. You may be asking, "Why 5 a.m.?" Well, it was to avoid any scheduling conflicts with classes. Our practice was from 12 to 4 p.m., which meant sometimes teammates had to arrive late or leave early to get to class on time; however, this was never a problem at 5 a.m. We would get up as a team to run along the river, do sprints on the football field, or run laps around the track. No matter what the cardio was, we knew everyone on the team would be there (even the injured ones) to bond and demonstrate that we were a team. If we could get through cardio mornings, have class, practice, and get back to class, then we could conquer anything together!

In addition to conditioning, during college, a lot of time was spent in the training room. This was for rehabilitation (to fix injuries), prehabilitation (to prevent injuries), and general body repair. I had a love-hate relationship with ice baths, which were intended to reduce pain and inflammation. Besides helping to heal our bodies, ice baths became another way to bond. The ice baths were just big enough to fit three or four of us gymnasts in there. It would be a combination of shrieking, giggling, and pain, but it was another great bonding experience.

MENTORSHIP

Along with friendships, another social benefit of gymnastics is mentorship. You may or may not practice with people who are your age, but either way there are people older than you in the gym—either a fellow teammate or a coach. Even a teammate who is just a year or two older than you can often provide the best mentorship opportunities.

Mentorship can be as formal or informal as you like. You might connect through training together. Or you might bond over a specific skill that they are good at but you are struggling with, fears, or even something outside the gym, such as a hobby, an interest, or faith. Whatever the reason, you are surrounded by people who can provide advice. Mentorship can also continue even after you are done with gym.

The best-case scenario is having a mentor while also being a mentor yourself! Check out some of the benefits of mentorship in the table that follows.

Having a Mentor	Being a Mentor
• Resource of support and guidance • Opportunity to get advice • Gain new perspective • Hear critiques • Help build your confidence	• Build your leadership skills • Beneficial for team culture • Gain new perspective • Give back and enjoy a sense of fulfillment • Help build your confidence

HOW TO FIND A MENTOR

It may feel difficult or awkward to ask someone to be your mentor. Here are a few ideas on how to get started:

1. Think about who you think would be a good mentor for you. Who do you look up to? Who would you like to be in five or ten years?

2. Think about your goals (short-term and long-term) and if they overlap with someone else's achievements. Is there someone who is a very hard worker? Someone who has overcome great obstacles?

3. Have a plan of how you'll ask. Be clear about your goals and why you think this person would be a good mentor for you.

If you need a script, then try something like this:

Hi _____, I love watching your gymnastics and I was so inspired when you overcame [tearing your ACL to come back and then win states]. I have been struggling with [injuries, fears, and so on] and wanted to ask if you'd be willing to chat with me either in person or over the phone for [20 minutes a week] to mentor me and help me overcome obstacles like you have.

Edit the script to fit your situation. Also, be aware that people are busy! The first person you ask might not have time right now—and that is fine! Don't take it personally. You can check back with them in six months or see if there is someone else who could be a good fit.

COACH CONNECTION

Your teammates essentially become family from all the time spent together and the unique experiences you go through together. But many would argue that coaches also become family. You spend so much time with your coaches that they know you almost as well as your own parents do. When I was in high school, there was a year or two when my coach would pick my teammate and me up from school or the public transit center and take us to the gym. This meant we would spend an hour (or more, depending on traffic) together in the car every day.

One time I got in the car holding the report card I had just received. Although it wasn't a terrible report card, it wasn't as strong as it should have been. My coach talked to me about the value of doing well in school in order to earn a college scholarship. This made a lasting impact on me. I knew he was right. Although my parents had also talked to me about the value of good grades, it felt very different coming from someone who was communicating directly with college coaches and who had gotten many of his athletes college scholarships. I owe so many of my life skills and lessons to my coaches.

In addition to coaches being mentors and influential people who help us become better gymnasts and better people, there is another layer to the gymnast-coach relationship: spotting. While learning new skills, we often need to be spotted, which can sometimes mean putting your life in your coaches' hands. Additionally, coaches are in charge of setting the equipment to the appropriate height for the athlete on the bars and vault. Again, you must trust your coach to adjust the equipment to the proper setting, as well as tighten it, or else there could be serious consequences. This builds trust between you and your coach.

As I got older in the gym and earned leadership roles, my relationship with my coach also changed. My coach would still critique me and give me corrections, but he'd also ask for my opinion on certain matters related to the team. It might not sound significant, but this was very different from the teacher-student relationship that began when I was ten. Providing (at least some) advice regarding decisions felt empowering, in addition to continuing to foster my blooming leadership skills. It made me realize that I had experience and I was helpful in making decisions for the whole team.

I feel incredible gratitude to all the coaches I had over the years. They did not let me give up when I wanted to, they taught me respect and discipline, and they believed in me when I doubted myself.

It sometimes feels like I've lived multiple lives with my gym friends, mentors, and coaches. They knew me when I was a child, an adolescent, a college student, and now beyond. Gym friendships grow and change over the years, but gymnastics can create deep bonds and friendships that last a lifetime.

CHAPTER 6 KEY TAKEAWAYS

1. Gymnastics builds friendships from the amount of time spent together, as well as your unique shared experiences.

2. Strong friendships in childhood and adolescence are particularly beneficial for developing social and emotional skills and building self-esteem.

3. Gymnastics creates a sense of belonging, real connection, and social skills, such as teamwork, selflessness, trust, cooperation, and good communication.

4. Mentorship is invaluable; there are many benefits to both having a mentor and being a mentor.

5. Coaches are crucial to your training in that they spot you and provide corrections, but they also make you a better person by instilling respect and leadership values.

***

Now that we've covered all the best parts of gymnastics, in part 2 we are going to shift gears and look at some of the downsides and challenges that are just as much a part of the sport.

PART II

HANDLING THE HARDSHIPS OF GYMNASTICS

CHAPTER 7

TIME-CONSUMING

"There's a difference between interest and commitment. When you're interested in doing something, you do it only when circumstance permit. When you're committed to something, you accept no excuses, only results."

—Art Turock

author, athlete, speaker, and corporate consulting expert

Gymnastics takes up an incredible amount of time. Countless hours are spent driving to and from the gym, in practice, in rehabilitation, in prehabilitation, at competitions, in travel to and from competitions, not to mention the time spent at all the social activities related to gym friends, such as birthday parties, sleepovers, hangouts, and so on.

Most (nonprofessional) sports require one to two hours of practice a few days a week. To an athlete who is not a gymnast, this could feel like a big commitment; however, when you look at a gymnastics training schedule, there is no comparison. Gymnasts often practice between 20 and 30 hours a week, doubling or even tripling the training schedule of most other sports.

Because gymnastics is a year-round sport, there is no offseason, unlike most other sports. In summer, when most kids are going to camp or on vacation with their family, you are in the gym. In addition, your summer training schedule is often even longer than your normal 25-hour practice week. My summer schedule was 30 hours a week. Although in some ways summer practice is like going to camp every day, camps usually offer a range of activities, while practice is the same every day. We looked at the social benefits of gymnastics in chapter 6. Let's now take a look at the flip side of that: the social cost.

SOCIAL COST

We all get only so much time in a day. The amount of time dedicated to gym takes time away from social activities. This includes activities with school friends, dating, and building friendships outside gym or school.

SCHOOL FRIENDSHIPS

As we talked about in chapter 6, your high-intensity training schedule builds incredibly strong bonds with gym friends; however, this often means less time spent with school friends. Although there are benefits to having friends outside school, it is still important to have and maintain school friendships, because a good portion of your life is spent in school. Having school friends helps you have a better attitude toward education and learning by making you more engaged.[41]

Just as you are going through unique experiences training with gym friends, school is a foundation for its own core memories and social connections. Studies have also shown that working with people you like (solving problems with friends) allows you to learn more and perform better.[42]

Additionally, school friendships help with transitional times in your life. The transition from elementary to middle school or from middle school to high school can be stressful. Having school friends who are going through the same experience can make these transitions much smoother.

Another aspect of spending so much time in the gym is that jealousy is bound to happen. Maybe you are feeling behind in gym, and therefore feel frustrated with or jealous of your teammates. If your only social network is through gym, then this can feel like an even bigger issue. Having school friends can provide you with an outlet when gym is intense.

Finally, sometimes you change gyms. Although changing gyms doesn't mean you'll lose your current gym friendships, it still changes your relationships. It is helpful to have consistent school friends during a gym transition.

SOCIAL NETWORK

The time commitment of gymnastics also limits the number of friendships and relationships you can build outside gym or school. The benefits of enlarging your circle of friends beyond gym and school include expanding your sense of belonging and purpose, broadening your horizons, and having a greater variety of experiences. Having other friends grows your identity, so you are not defined as "the gymnast." Additionally, if you are having trouble with gym or school friends, then you have other people you can turn to.

Additionally, interacting with people outside school and gym means you will be exposed to different people and a greater range of diversity. In school, you are surrounded by people who live in the same geographic area. Gym allows you to interact with people outside your immediate area, but it is an expensive sport and therefore decreases the range of people you can meet. When you participate in local community teams and events, you can meet an even broader range of interesting, diverse people.

NO TIME FOR OTHER ACTIVITIES

In addition to gymnastics taking time away from growing your social connections, it also takes away time that could be spent playing other sports, learning other skills, or participating in other activities.

OTHER SPORTS

Although gymnastics makes you more coordinated and better at other sports, when all your time is dedicated to gymnastics, you never get the chance to try other sports! Although many of your friends are on travel soccer teams or baseball, softball, or dance teams, with your training schedule, on top of competitions, there is no time left over.

And although it's great to be really good at one sport, there are also many benefits to trying different sports, like the ones mentioned in this chapter, to see if you like another sport better or see what other sports you are good at.

1. **Team dynamics:** When you try different sports, you are exposed to different team dynamics. For example, although gymnastics is both a team and an individual sport, your performance and score rest solely in your hands. In other sports, you can't score points or make goals without teammates passing you the ball or blocking defenders. It's important to learn how to rely on and trust in others in order to have success.

2. **Overuse injury prevention:** Training other sports also works different muscle groups to help prevent overuse injuries. Gymnastics puts stress on all muscles, but as you can imagine, certain muscle groups are strained more often. By doing other sports, you use different muscle groups to (it is hoped) prevent overuse injuries.

Training other sports can also benefit your gymnastics. For example, gymnastics doesn't require as much cardio as running or swimming. When you practice endurance-based sports, you are building up your cardiovascular system, which actually makes your more cardio-intense routines (such as the floor) much easier.

3. **Maintain interest:** Because there is really no downtime in gymnastics, your training schedule can become repetitive. Every week is the same schedule, day in and day out; you are bound to feel bored at some point. If you practice or learn another sport, then it pushes you, both mentally and physically, which can be exciting and interesting.

Research has also shown that kids who specialize in a sport at a young age are actually more inclined to quit, due to factors such as decreased motivation and loss of enjoyment.[43] Having a breadth of sports that you have experience with and are good at gives you more choices as you get older.

Playing other sports can also help prevent burnout, which is common in gymnastics. Training other sports can lower the stakes in gym and can refresh your mindset.

4. **Transferable skills:** Another benefit of doing multiple sports is that many skills learned in one sport are directly transferable to other sports. Although gymnastics helps with overall athleticism, learning different sports helps develop movement skills and increases physical literacy,

which is defined as "the ability, motivation, and knowledge to be physically active for life."[44] From doing a range of sports, you can see the countless ways to continue to be active outside gymnastics.

Gymnastics is generally not a sport you can do when you get older (although there are some extraordinary exceptions; check out the sidebar below). On the other hand, there are many sports that you can do (and are common) well into older age, such as running, swimming, soccer, tennis, dancing, and golf. Training different sports when you are younger allows you to more easily learn or continue these sports when you are older.

AGELESS GYMNASTS

Although the cutoff age to be a competitive gymnast is usually around 21 or 22, with the end of college gymnastics, there are some exceptions to this that defy all odds.

Johanna Quaas is a German gymnast who was born in 1925 and at the age of 92 was still actively competing! In April, 2012 Quaas was certified by Guinness World Records as the world's oldest active competitive gymnast.[45] Another exceptional example is the gymnast from Uzbekistan, Oksana Chusovitina (born in 1975), who has competed at *eight* Olympic games.[46] She competed at the 2020 Tokyo games at the age of 45 and is still competing at the highest level at 48 years old!

OTHER SKILLS

Outside sports, it is beneficial to have a range of skills that you can use for future jobs, hobbies, and social connection. Following are a few examples of these skills.

1. **Computer skills and programming skills:** Spending the time to learn computer and programming skills can be extremely beneficial in getting a job and having general computer knowledge.

2. **Language skills:** Being able to speak another language is helpful for traveling, getting jobs, and general mental stimulation.

3. **Cooking:** Cooking is a passion for many people. Being able to cook is a great way to create healthy lifestyle habits, bring people together to create community, and indulge in different flavors.

4. **Self-defense:** Not only is self-defense beneficial for your safety, but also it is a fun and unique physical training activity.

5. **Do-it-yourself skills:** This can range from building your own furniture to hanging pictures to repairing broken chairs. Even mechanical skills fall into this category.

6. **Money management:** Another skill that is very useful is learning how to budget and manage your money. There are countless training courses, blogs, and books that provide a wealth of information on the subject.

OTHER ACTIVITIES

There are also many activities that you don't have time for when so much time is spent in the gym. Taking part in these activities, such as those in the list that follows, make you a more well-rounded person:

1. **Acting classes, drama club:** Taking acting classes or being part of a drama club can sharpen your acting skills and increase your social connections.

2. **Art:** Spending time with your creative side can be a great outlet.

3. **Community service:** Community service allows you to give back to your community and makes you feel good.

4. **Poetry, writing:** Writing allows you to create other worlds.

5. **Student council:** Student council is an excellent way to develop your leadership skills and strengthen a college application.

6. **Music:** Music activities can range from joining a choir to taking singing lessons, learning an instrument, or joining a band.

7. **Comedy:** If you enjoy stand-up comedy, then you might want to take an improvisational comedy class or write your own jokes!

8. **Religion:** Affiliation with a religious institution can be a great way to deepen your faith, become more involved in your community, and grow your social connections.

BROADEN YOUR IDENTITY

Because gymnastics takes so much of your time, your identity may be wrapped up in gymnastics. That is a lot of pressure! If you don't do well in a competition or if you're struggling at gym, then it feels like your world is falling apart. If you have other skills or activities that you are involved in (and are good at), then you have a better perspective. Gymnastics is what you do; it is not who you are.

NO TIME FOR OTHER EXPERIENCES

In addition to not having the time to try other activities, there are certain life experiences that you aren't able to partake in. Let's look at a few.

TRAVEL

The time constraints and year-round schedule of gymnastics leave little time for travel or vacations. Travel is important to be able to experience other countries, cultures, and people. Although there is some travel in gymnastics, it is mostly domestic travel and there usually isn't much time to explore. Instead, you are traveling from the airport to the hotel, and from there to the competition, and then it's back to the airport to fly home. There are many benefits to traveling: seeing how other people live, experiencing other cultures, getting out of your comfort zone, and enjoying new experiences.

JOBS AND INTERNSHIPS

Your intense training schedule takes away from other common experiences, especially as you get older. For example, it is common to get summer jobs or internships toward the end of high school and in college. Spending six hours a day in the gym, usually during the middle of the day, can make this challenging. Summer jobs are a great way to earn money, acquire foundational work skills, gain experience, and network with coworkers. It is difficult to have a job on top of your training schedule, not only because of time constraints but also because you are most likely exhausted after practice. You have only so much time and energy in a day.

During my high school summers, I worked as a lifeguard at the local pool after practice most days. Not only did I have to plan my work schedule carefully so it didn't interfere with gym, but also I had to make sure I got enough sleep and planned out my meals so I could keep up with both commitments.

Additionally, when I was in college, most of my peers had summer internships to prepare them for the working world. But I was not able to get an internship because of my gym training schedule. Although an internship isn't essential, there are certainly benefits to the experience and to the networking opportunities.

STUDY ABROAD

For many, studying abroad is a highlight of their college years. You get to live in a different country, experience the day-to-day life of its people, learn a new language, enjoy local food, and meet new people. A semester abroad is most likely not in the cards if you are looking to compete in college. The fall semester in college includes training in the gym, getting stronger in the weight room, team bonding, and practice competitions in order to prepare for the spring semester, which is the gymnastics competition season. It's not possible to take a few weeks off practice for a vacation, let alone an entire semester abroad. Although I loved my college experience, I wish I could have experienced studying abroad.

TIME WITH FAMILY

Gymnastics also takes away from family time. Growing up, one of my favorite activities was eating dinner with my family; however, this rarely happened because I was always at practice during dinnertime. Additionally, the intense training schedule and the philosophy of "no good time to take time off" limit the time available for family vacations. The time pressure experienced by a gymnast is so great that it is not uncommon for a gymnast and one parent—or even the entire family—to move so the gymnast can be closer to a specific training center or train with a well-regarded coach.

BURNOUT

Regardless of how much you love gymnastics, spending that much time doing anything can often lead to burnout: you feel worn down or exhausted from a specific activity or stress. Not only is the extensive training physically demanding but also it causes mental exhaustion. You never get a break!

In gym, every minute of every day is spoken for. You are in school or in the car or in the gym—or you are either eating on the run or doing homework. Maybe you love being busy, but you can do only so much before you are physically and mentally drained. This is common in gymnastics.

When you reach burnout, your body, mind, and energy are spent. Burnout is one of the most common reasons for quitting gymnastics. To avoid burnout, maintain a balanced life. Take breaks, take vacations, and take time off for life events. You shouldn't need to miss out on everything. Also, make sure you are fueling yourself enough to keep going. This means good sleep, eating enough, and eating food that will nourish you (discussed in chapter 9). Other ways to renew yourself mentally are meditation, journaling, and spending time outside. Also, make sure you ask for help when you need it. Lean on your teammates, coaches, parents, school counselors, or other family members.

Some gyms do a great job of adding games and changing assignments to make practice fun but also exciting and varied. See if your coach is willing to create different assignments to make each event more fun and engaging.

SLEEP

As you know, sleep is vital for your mental and physical well-being, for your athletic performance, and for your general happiness. So when every moment of every day is filled with an activity and you don't get home until 9:30 p.m. and then have to turn around and do homework, getting enough sleep can certainly be a challenge.

Additionally, after practice, your mind may be all wound up because you got in trouble with your coach, had a conflict with a teammate, felt a lingering fear, experienced worry about school...the list goes on. It may not be easy to drift off to sleep, even though you feel exhausted. Having to excel in the gym, at school, and with friends, and not having enough time to dedicate to all of them can be a huge stressor. This stress can become a vicious cycle. Because you are stressed, you don't sleep well or long enough. Then because you didn't sleep well or long enough, you aren't as equipped to handle the stress.

There is no simple solution for the lack of sleep, but as much as you can, try to keep some separation between what happens in the gym and what happens outside the gym. Do your best to keep your gym thoughts in the gym (maybe even in the car ride home, if you need to vent), but after that, let them go and move on to the next thing.

Having a routine to wind down after a long day or chaotic afternoon can also help you get in the right headspace before sleep. If you lie down and immediately notice your thoughts going wild, then try to be mindful of those thoughts and take deep breaths to get to a calmer place. Also, remember that there is nothing you can do about practice now, so there is no need to keep replaying what happened or stressing about what's to come. Realize you can control only so much, and tomorrow is a new day to face those challenges.

ANOTHER PERSPECTIVE

Usain Bolt said something that I'm constantly reminded of when thinking about the time commitment of gymnastics. He said, "I trained four years to run nine seconds, and people give up when they don't see results in two months."[47] People want incredible results without the time commitment, which is never possible.

There is no getting around the massive time commitment required by gymnastics. The time commitment helps you with your time management skills and makes you focus on what is truly important; however, it also means less time for friends outside the gym, other sports or activities, or your family. Remember why you chose gymnastics, and try to maximize the fun and enjoyment in the gym every day.

ASK THE EXPERT: DR. ALISON ARNOLD

Dr. Alison Arnold, MS, PhD, is a mental toughness coach and founder of Head Games. Doc Ali, as she is known, shares her views on how to work through the difficultness of the time commitment of gymnastics.

"Although the time commitment of gymnastics is a lot to ask, to be extraordinary, you need to put in extraordinary effort. On the other hand, it's also important to remember to maintain balance in your life. Keeping balance means making sure your battery is still charged in order to put in the energy required to be a great athlete. If your battery is depleted, you won't be able to do your best. Feed yourself with what brings you joy and fuels you. You could be fueled by friendships, music, hobbies, a spiritual life. Whatever it is, make sure you are still feeding that part of you.

"There is always going to be a big time commitment to be successful at anything, but maintaining balance is just as important. Find what brings you joy with life outside the gym. When you put too much weight on gym, there is too much pressure on you. You are more than just a gymnast. You are a human being and have so much to offer."

CHAPTER 7 KEY TAKEAWAYS

1. The time commitment of gymnastics is one of the common reasons for quitting the sport.

2. The amount of time spent in the gym takes away time from other activities, including socializing, learning other sports, acquiring other skills, and time with family.

3. There are benefits to trying other sports, including being part of different team dynamics, overuse injury prevention, maintaining interest in gymnastics, and learning other transferable skills.

4. Burnout is common in gymnastics because the sport can be mentally and physically exhausting. To overcome burnout, take breaks if possible, get enough sleep, fuel your body, write in your journal, and lean on friends and family.

5. To be great at anything, you need to put in an incredible amount of time. Gymnastics makes you manage your time better, and focuses your energy on the things you truly love.

CHAPTER 8

FEAR

"Fear is only as deep as the mind allows."

—Japanese proverb

A frequent obstacle and one of the most common reasons for quitting gymnastics is fear. In this chapter we will focus on where fear comes from, different ways fear manifests itself, and ways to work with and overcome your fears.

Sometimes fear is based on one skill, and sometimes it's a few skills or an entire event when fear takes over. Fear can happen when you're learning a skill or after you've done it for years. Fear can show up differently for different athletes, but it is always frustrating and disheartening.

So what can you do? Let's start with where fear comes from.

WHY DO YOU HAVE FEAR?

Fear can come from many places and is a natural response of the body to avoid physical or mental pain, embarrassment, or letting someone down. You can gradually develop a fear through a fall or fear can seem to appear out of nowhere.

As you get older, fear starts to creep in more. You realize how crazy gymnastics is! You also think about the consequences if you fall or if the skill doesn't go as planned. These are thoughts that you didn't have as much when you were younger. Also, when you're younger, you can get spotted on a skill, and it's easy for your coach to lift you and carry you through the skill. As you grow, this becomes more difficult, and learning new skills becomes more trial and error on your own.

Maybe you've done a skill for years and have never had any fears. Then all of a sudden, you develop a fear that blocks you. You are feeling frustrated and wondering why this is happening, seemingly out of nowhere. Anna Kojac, an online mental gymnastics coach, does a great job of explaining fear in her *Stick It Girl* blog. She explains that your brain is "hard-wired differently than when [you're] older." When you are younger, your brain is making lots of new connections, which allow you to learn skills and abilities. "Around ages 10–13 (adolescence) a switch starts to take place. One of the big things that happens during this time is that the unused connections in the grey matter of [your] brain are pruned away. Likewise, the connections that are used the most are further strengthened and solidified. It's a 'use it or lose it' sort of thing." [48] The brain starts clearing away connections that aren't used to make the brain more efficient." This clearing starts at the back of the brain where there is something called the amygdala. The amygdala is responsible for controlling emotions and behavior, including fear, anxiety, and depression.[49] What all this means is that your brain becomes more aware of danger with age, and therefore having a fear response will be more common than before.

Another reason you may experience fear is a bad experience. Maybe you hurt yourself or you saw someone else get hurt doing the same skill. It is understandable and normal to feel like this; however, it's also important to know that messing up and falling is a part of gymnastics. Just because you got hurt or you saw someone else get hurt does not mean that it will happen again or that you will get hurt. It could have been a fluke turn. For example, you walk around all the time, but on occasion, you trip, right? Well, it's the same in gym. You do all your skills perfectly fine the majority of the time, but on occasion, you will have a fall, mess up, or trip. That shouldn't define how you look at yourself or the skill. This is normal and part of the learning process.

TYPES OF FEAR

Along with your brain maturing or you having a bad experience, there are plenty of other reasons for having fears. These include the fear of failure, fear of success, fear of embarrassment, fear of disappointment—and the list goes on. These are all valid reasons for fear.

FEAR OF FAILURE

Failure is a fundamental part of gymnastics and an inherent part of life. Failures set you up for future success. So give it a shot. You might succeed or fail, but either way you are moving in the right direction and are one step closer to success.

FEAR OF SUCCESS

Fear of success means you might be consciously (or unconsciously) afraid that you might perform this skill once but won't be able to do it again. Maybe you have a fear that you won't be able to keep succeeding as skills become more difficult. If you have these thoughts, then remember that you are skipping ahead many steps! You are stressing about things that are so far away and out of your control right now. Instead of thinking about what *could* happen, stay in the present. Take things one step at a time. Focus on the one skill at hand. Then focus on the next skill and then the next. There is no need to jump ahead and get concerned about things that may or may not happen in the future.

FEAR OF EMBARRASSMENT

If you have a fear of embarrassment, then the main thing you should know about feeling embarrassed is that no one cares as much as you think they do! People are thinking about themselves the majority of the time. We think people care about what we do much more than they really do. What may feel completely embarrassing or like the end of the world to you, is something that someone else may have barely even noticed. Also, realize that everyone makes mistakes and messes up. This is how we learn and get better.

Another strategy to overcome fear of embarrassment is to humiliate yourself intentionally. It may sound silly, but if you are brave enough, then it just might work for you! Whatever your most embarrassing scenario is, make that happen, and then you'll realize it wasn't as bad as you expected.

FEAR OF DISAPPOINTMENT

Another extremely common fear is the fear of disappointing others: your coach, peers, family, and so on. Whoever it is, know that you are doing this sport for *you* and no one else. When you are afraid to disappoint others, it often comes from your self-worth being tied to the thing you do. Although it may feel like gymnastics is your full identity, *you have so much more to offer than just being a good gymnast.* You may not feel worthy if you disappoint others, but I am here to tell you that you *are* worthy, exactly as you are, with every mistake you've ever made. That success will make you proud of yourself, as well as those others whom you were afraid of disappointing.

THE MANIFESTATION OF FEAR

Now that we've covered why fear develops and some different types of fear, let's get into how fear manifests, specifically in gymnastics.

BALKING

You may have heard the term *to balk* before, but if you haven't or you've never experienced it yourself, then consider yourself lucky! Balking is when a gymnast has a fear of a skill and because of that fear refuses to attempt the skill or even stops in the middle of it. It may be a rare occurrence—maybe the gymnast balks once out of a dozen turns—but if the fear progresses, then that gymnast may start balking more and more frequently. It is a vicious cycle, as you can see in the following graphic.

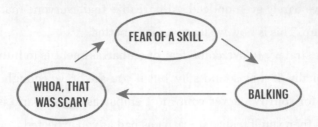

After balking a few times, you may fear balking more than the actual skill. When you stop yourself partway through a skill it feels like you don't have control over your body or mind. You may try to avoid the skill completely for fear of balking.

I have plenty of memories of myself balking. One that particularly stands out was learning a back handspring on the high beam. One time I started to flip and then froze in midair. I ended up landing flat on my back on the beam and then rolling off. It wasn't pretty. I tell this story because it is a common and normal experience in gymnastics. To avoid balking in the future, it's helpful to think about why you are balking and then how you can fix it.

Why Are You Balking?

When balking happens, first try to assess why. There could be a perfectly logical reason.

1. Do you feel like you don't have the strength or ability to do this?

2. Do you feel rushed into doing this skill?

3. Do you have outside stress that is getting in the way?

4. Is the fear of balking scarier than the actual skill?

How to Fix It

To overcome the fear, lower the stakes. In my case, it meant going down to back handsprings on the floor, and then the floor beam, and slowly building back my confidence until I could try again on the high beam. Break the skill down as much as you can to slowly get back to where you want it to be. This may involve getting a spot or going into the pit. Do whatever you can to remind your body and brain that you are able to do the skill. Take your time and try different ways to progress to the actual skill. Repeat the skill on any surface where you don't balk, and keep doing this again and again. The goal is to get the feeling of balking out of your mind until you can get back to focusing on the skill.

Another important part of getting through this experience is not getting frustrated. This is always easier said than done. Not getting frustrated is important for the athlete, coach, and parents involved. You have to work with your mind and find which approach succeeds. Getting frustrated adds more stress to an already difficult situation. So take a few deep breaths and then break the skill down to its smaller and easier parts.

Your parents or coaches may want to help by talking you through the fear. This could make the situation either better or worse. Depending on the skill, sometimes talking through what was going on in my mind made it seem not so bad; however, sometimes talking about it would make my fear grow. Figure out what works for you.

THE TWISTIES

Another common occurrence in gymnastics is the dreaded twisties. This is when you lose your normal twisting or visual cues and get disoriented in the air. Hardly anyone is immune to the terrible twisties! Simone Biles publicly talked about her experience getting the twisties during the 2020 Olympics and having to back out of some of the events.

How to Fix It

It is an awful feeling to not know where you are in the air and not know how many flips or twists you've done. Simone Biles shared with *Time* magazine how she "couldn't tell up from down and had no idea if she was going to land on [her] hands, head, feet, back or what."[50] To recover from the twisties, she had to withdraw from the competition to focus on getting back to basics. And it's the same process for you. Get back to basics, just like with balking.

Don't let stress or confusion take over. Accept that this is a part of the sport, and everyone goes through it at some point. Even Simone Biles, the greatest gymnast of all time! So take a few deep breaths, and then go back to step one.

If you are messing up a double twist, then start with a layout into the pit. Then maybe a full, then a one and a half, and so on. Work your way back to feeling your regular cues again. It may take a few days or even a few weeks. Sometimes the best option is giving yourself a mental break and coming back the next day. Remember the three B's: breathe, break down, and then break through.

MENTAL BLOCKS

A similar fear-based aversion is having a mental block. A mental block is when your body prevents you from even attempting a skill. This can also feel like you have no control over your own body. Mentally, you are ready to go, but your body pumps the brakes.

I had a mental block when I tried learning a Tkatchev on bars. There was something about the movement of a Tkatchev that didn't make sense in my mind. You have to move backward while turning your body forward. My coach was all ready to spot me on the single rail, but when I got to the top of the swing, I wouldn't let go of the bar. My mind and words were saying, "I'm ready to try it," but my body didn't agree.

How to Fix It

As with balking and the twisties, to overcome a mental block, get back to what feels safe. I had to go back to the Tkatchev drills I had been practicing. If going back to basics helps you get over your mental block, then that's great. For me, it still didn't click, so I decided to learn a different release move that I could make my body go for.

I had a teammate who had a general fear of going backward, particularly back handsprings. Your initial reaction may be that there's no way you can do gymnastics if you won't go backward. I am here to tell you that it is possible! On each event she found a way to do only forward-facing skills. (That said, on the floor, you need to have at least one backward element, so she did a standing back tuck—but that was it.) If you have a similar fear that prohibits you from doing a skill or even going in a specific direction, then you can in fact compete all-around (and compete as a college athlete) even with this mental block. You may have to make some tweaks to your routines to satisfy the requirements on each event, but you can make it work!

With mental blocks, you can either work to overcome them or figure out ways to work around them.

ASK THE EXPERT: DR. ALISON ARNOLD

Dr. Alison Arnold, MS, PhD (Doc Ali), shares some similes related to mental blocks in gymnastics.

"Think of your brain like a highway. The goal is to create a smooth road from where you currently are to the skill you are working on. Use breathing and positive self-talk to lay the foundation for your road. Next, use key words to keep your mind locked in on only this one road. Don't let your mind get off course. Next, practice successful repetitions and progressions to continue to smooth that road. It's important not to train balking. Balking is like adding sticks and rocks to your road. It ruins the smooth path that you're building and you have to go back a step to smooth out the road. Finally, be in a good mental state before you take your turn. Your mind needs to be locked down in order to run good progressions to create a good mental pathway."

or

"You can also think of your brain like a bank. You can either make deposits or withdrawals. Deposits are when you have positive experiences (a successful turn) and withdrawals are negative experiences (like balking). As with a real bank, you want to have more deposits than withdrawals. Optimally, you will have lots of deposits (positive experiences), so when you do have to make a withdrawal (a negative experience), that single withdrawal won't deplete all the deposits you have. It's important to have a solid foundation of deposits to face any withdrawals that you may encounter."

YOUR BRAIN IN FEAR

Now that we know what fear is and some of the different ways fear manifests itself, we are going to talk about the way fear affects your physical state.

Fear can take over your body and mind if you let it, as you know with balking, the twisties, and mental blocks. When you feel fear, your body enters a fight-or-flight state, which includes an increased heart rate, tensed muscles, and shortness of breath. Your body is preparing itself to either fight or run. Brian Cain, a mental performance coach and author, says that "our bodies are not meant to sustain this state. Most of all, athletes will not be able to perform well under these sympathetic nervous system conditions."[51] When you are in this state, your mental and physical training seems to go out the window and you feel like you have no control.

Fear is your brain's reaction to the crazy skills you are doing. Fear is telling your body to *stay alert because crazy things are happening*. Which is true! What you are practicing in the gym, the skills you are training, are not usual things for the body to be doing. Your brain is simply trying to figure out what is going on. How do you work with fear? That discussion follows.

WORKING WITH FEAR

When your body is in this tense fear state, the first thing you need to do is calm your brain. Take deep breaths to calm the amygdala, turn off fight-or-flight mode, and decrease the activity of the sympathetic nervous system. Also, be aware of how you are holding your face and what your body language looks and feels like. If your face and body are still tense, then it will be harder to convince your brain that everything is all right. Loosen those muscles in your face, hands, shoulders, and so on. Once you are physically in a calmer state, remember not to be too hard on yourself. Understand that fear is an indication that your brain needs you to work some tools to feel confident again. Next, let's overcome that fear.

OVERCOMING FEAR

Instead of succumbing to your fears, try these steps to overcome your fears.

Take some deep breaths: With fear we often make it a bigger deal than it actually is and work ourselves up. The first step is to take a few deep breaths and calm yourself down. This helps the brain become more rational too. Breathe in through your nose for seven seconds, and breathe out through your mouth for eight seconds. This deep breathing will calm your mind and your physical reactions as well.

State the facts: When you are in a state of fear, it may feel like your mind is going a million miles an hour. Along with deep breathing, start telling yourself facts, instead of *what if* situations. For example, tell yourself, "I have trained for this. I am ready" or "I know my breathing cues and how to get my heart rate down. I know how to make adjustments when needed." These are just examples of what facts you can say. Think of some of your own as well, whatever will get you to a place where you believe what you are saying and you are able to be in control of your body and mind.

Also, talk to yourself about what is actually happening. When your heart rate is up and you feel fear, your body doesn't know whether you are walking into competition or going to fight a bear. Your body just knows that it's scared. Acknowledge that you are going to a competition, but point out that this is not a life-or-death situation.

Positive self-talk: The next step is to focus on how you are talking to or about yourself. If you are telling yourself that you are stupid or a baby for having fear, then you need to *stop*. Change that self-talk. You are doing incredibly challenging skills that most people couldn't even imagine doing! That is impressive and worth acknowledging. Finally, imagine what you would say to a teammate to encourage them. You'd probably say something along the lines of, "You can do this" or "You are capable." Then say those phrases to yourself!

Verbal cues: Another way to keep your mind focused is with verbal cues. You can either say your cues aloud or say them in your head. These cues can be corrections that your coach has given you or your own cues that help you stay focused. As I mentioned in chapter 1, sometimes I'd even sing to myself so I wouldn't be thinking about fear or entertaining negative thoughts.

Back to basics: If your fear is of doing something on the high beam or a skill without mats, then get back to your basics. Think about how you first learned the skill. You probably started with drills on the floor or in the pit and slowly built up to using the actual equipment. You might not need to go all the way back to the floor, but go back at least a few steps or progressions until you feel confident again. It's also important to note that going back to basics is not a punishment; rather, it's a way to enhance self-assurance.

Build your confidence: Along with positive self-talk and building up skills on lower mats until you feel confident, think about how amazing you are for all the skills you *can do*. Think about all the times you've learned and performed skills successfully. You are talented, strong, and able to do this! If you need more ideas on building your self-confidence, then check out page 80 in chapter 5.

Visualize: It may take a few tries, but a great way to work with your fears is to imagine and visualize yourself doing the skill, whether it's something you've done hundreds of times or something you're currently learning. Think about exactly what it would look and feel like to do the skill successfully.

Write It Out

Write down some examples of facts you can tell yourself to calm yourself when you feel fear.

Example: "I know how to do this skill or routine." Or "I am capable of adapting to any situation."

_____

_____

Write down examples of verbal cues that you can say to yourself to stay focused.

Example: "Stay tight, equal arms, push through."

_____

_____

Having fears consumes a lot of your physical and mental energy. Try one or all of the preceding techniques and see if you notice a difference. Whether this is a skill you have done a hundred times or you are trying it for the first time, having fears is normal; however, you have the ability to train your mind and body to overcome this fear. Remember to be kind to yourself and know that overcoming fears will make you a better gymnast, athlete, and person.

Using coping mechanisms, such as those discussed, has been shown to benefit your gymnastics. Scott B. Martin et al. did a study on anxiety experienced during competitive gymnastics and found that gymnasts who got further in terms of level and skill were the ones who used more fear-coping strategies than the less skilled gymnasts.[52] So at least give these suggestions a try and see what happens.

LEAN ON OTHERS

When you are experiencing fear, lean on others to help you through it. This could mean talking with teammates who have had similar fears or who can offer advice. Sometimes just having a compassionate ear to listen to you can be the most effective solution.

Also, lean on your coach. You are not the first athlete who has had this particular fear, and you won't be the last. See if your coach has any suggestions for you. Or maybe they have drills or can spot you to build your confidence again. Your coach can't read your mind; if they don't know what's going on, then they can't help you. So communicate your thoughts.

Your coach also wouldn't make you do a skill that they didn't think you were ready for. Remember, coaches often see things in you that you aren't able to see in yourself. They know that you are fully capable of doing the skill physically, but sometimes it's your mind that seems to get in the way.

Fears are completely normal and part of the learning process of gymnastics. Don't get down on yourself. Don't beat yourself up. Be kind and patient, and use the tools in this chapter to build back your confidence and conquer your fears.

CHAPTER 8 KEY TAKEAWAYS

1. Fear is a normal part of gymnastics, but is one of the main reasons why people quit the sport.

2. Fears often start to pop up between ages 10 and 13 due to normal developmental changes in the brain.

3. Balking, the twisties, and mental blocks are mental obstacles that are often fear-based.

4. When you feel fear, your mind and body go into fight-or-flight mode. Calm your mind and body in order to get back in the driver's seat.

5. To overcome your fears, try taking deep breaths, stating the facts, positive self-talk, verbal cues, getting back to basics, building back your confidence, and visualizations.

CHAPTER 9

BODY DYSMORPHIA

"Hating your body will never get you as far as loving it will."

—**Unknown**

An innate part of the sport of gymnastics is how you look when you perform. There is so much focus on having perfect lines, a dramatic toe point, and a thin or muscular figure. This emphasis on how you look, rather than just your performance, is one of the most obvious reasons why body dysmorphia, eating disorders, and disordered eating are so common in the gymnastics world.

In this chapter, we are going to dive into the reasons why these conditions develop, hear from gymnasts who have dealt with them, and discuss ways to work with and overcome them.

THE FOUNDATION

To discuss body dysmorphia in gymnastics, we first must offer a few definitions. Body dysmorphia, or body dysmorphic disorder, is a mental health disorder in which you are "so worried about the way your body looks that it interferes with your ability to function normally."[53] When we talk about eating disorders, they are "severe disturbances in people's eating behaviors and related thoughts and emotions."[54] The most common examples of eating disorders are anorexia nervosa (usually referred to as anorexia), which is extreme caloric restriction, and bulimia nervosa (often just called bulimia), which is overeating and then self-inducing vomiting.

Disordered eating is a much broader term, meaning general "irregular eating, such as skipping meals, binge eating, using laxatives, diet pills, etc."[55] Disordered eating can also entail completely avoiding certain food groups.

There are a few reasons why these disorders are so prevalent in gymnastics. Unlike most sports, gymnastics is both performance-based and appearance-based, with results determined by a judge. Sports that are solely performance-based determine the winner by the number of points scored, time elapsed, and so on. For example, in swimming, the person who wins is the one who reaches the end of the pool first. In weight lifting, the person who lifts the most weight is declared the winner. In soccer, the team who scores the most goals wins. You get the idea. It doesn't matter what you look like, All that matters is how fast you are, how much weight you can lift, or how many points you can score. In gymnastics and other subjective sports (for example, ice skating or dance), not only do you have to perform your skills flawlessly, but also you are supposed to look a certain way while doing it. Although judges attempt to be objective and focus only on the skills, they are still human and can be influenced by the way someone looks. Gymnasts are often conditioned to think they need to look a certain way (that is, small and thin) to be successful in the eyes of the judge, as well as the coach. This is true for both women and men.

In addition to external pressure from judges, coaches, or peers to be a certain size, the fact that leotards and clothes worn in the gym are so skimpy and tight makes you even more aware of your body. The brevity and tightness of leotards and spandex is intended to allow you to move easily and safely, but this also means they show every inch of fat, cellulite, or stretch marks. Not only that, seeing yourself in these tight, unforgiving outfits daily can be particularly difficult when your body is growing and changing during adolescence.

REINFORCEMENT

If gymnastics attire does not already make you acutely aware of your body, the fact that how you look is a constant focus—as evidenced by comments and correction—is bound to affect you.

I have heard coaches say things like, "Lighter flies higher," "You must be thin to win," or other offhand comments about how being smaller is better. A college teammate of mine shared how her earlier coaches would make her teammates stick out their bellies as much as they could and then chastise those with the biggest bellies. There are countless stories of gymnasts being called names or put down for their weight. For example, the late Christy Henrich's coach allegedly compared her to the Pillsbury Doughboy; Katelyn Ohashi, a former US National team member and UCLA gymnast, was compared to a bird that was too fat to lift itself off the ground; and even Simone Biles shared in her memoir, *Courage to Soar*, that her coach said that "maybe if she didn't look like she swallowed a deer, she wouldn't have fallen." These are just a few of many disturbing examples.

I have a vivid memory from high school of when I went on a family vacation to Cambodia and Vietnam. When I came back from the trip, for whatever reason (maybe the food, heat, or amount of walking we did), I was significantly lighter. Although my coach had been very unhappy that I would miss practice for three weeks, when I came back smaller, he was more than pleased. "Maybe you should go on trips more often," he said, implying that going away on a trip was a great way to shed a few pounds. Although the comment was lighthearted and I tried not to take it personally, it sticks out in my memory. Every time I'd go on vacation after that, there would be some glimmer of hope that maybe I would in fact lose some weight on the trip, which would make up for my absence from the gym. Looking back on that mindset I had (around the age of fourteen) is disturbing for multiple reasons. First, it is great to take time off to let your mind and body rest, and more important, to see that there is a world outside gymnastics. Second, although it is important to eat well and have a balanced diet all the time, on vacation, I shouldn't be worrying about gaining weight that I'll have to shed once I'm back in the gym. Finally, as long as I can still do my skills, then it shouldn't matter if I am either a bit bigger or smaller after time away.

Another reason eating disorders seem to creep into gymnastics is because weight can sometimes feel like the only thing within your control. So much of gymnastics involves you being told what to do, how to do it, and what you're doing wrong. When it feels like there are so many things you can't control, being a certain weight or controlling what you eat might be the only way to feel some sense of control over your life.

THE "PERFECT" ATHLETE BODY

When looking at professional athletes, Olympians, or even teammates and fellow athletes, it's so easy to think that they all have "perfect" bodies. This body type usually includes toned legs and arms, a flat stomach (probably with abs), a muscular butt (that isn't too big), and so on. We may see someone competing on TV and think, "That's what I want to look like" or "That's what I *should* look like."

As a gymnast, you know that your body looks different from other people's. Particularly around middle school or high school age, others have gone through puberty and maybe you haven't. It may feel like you're not curvy enough, you're too short, or that you don't fill out your clothes like everyone else. Then all of a sudden, things change. You gain weight, have bulky muscles, and fill out your clothes, but not in a pretty, feminine way, as you had hoped. Your muscles and body may seem almost too masculine. Then you have people tell you, "You're so jacked" or maybe "You're so ripped" or possibly "You're so swole." Their words are usually intended as compliments, but as a girl, it may not feel like praise. So you decide that to be more feminine, you must get rid of that manly muscle and become thin. People have different experiences, but this is one way eating disorders begin. Does this sound familiar? This is the story of a former teammate of mine, whom we will hear more about.

The truth is, *there is no perfect body*—in gymnastics or elsewhere. Everyone needs to fuel their body differently, and even if you ate and exercised exactly the same as someone else, the two of you would not look the same. There are so many types of bodies, and all can do incredible things.

There is also a big difference in the way people put on muscle. College was the first time I ever weight lifted. For me, weight lifting caused me to put on solid, dense muscle. Other teammates who were also lifting weights for the first time put on much leaner muscle, which to my eyes looked better and more feminine. We were all becoming stronger, better gymnasts, but it looked very different for each person.

COMPARISON

Another factor contributing to body image issues in gymnastics is comparison. This could be you comparing yourself with other teammates or athletes. Or it might be your coach comparing you with others or even comparing how you look now versus how you used to look. Although comparison is not always a bad thing, if it makes you feel bad, then it is not healthy. Instead of focusing on what you don't have, think about where your strengths lie. Maybe you're not as skinny as your teammate, but that means you can tumble higher. Or maybe you're not as strong as someone else, but you are more flexible and can do impressive leaps. Whatever the situation is, you have your body type and there's nothing you can do about it. Focus on what you do have instead of wishing for what others have.

If the comparison is coming from your coach, then that is tougher to block out. After all, they're your coach and you're supposed to listen to what they say. Well, I say this is different, and you should block them out! You still want to be respectful, but you know that there is no ideal gymnast body, so try your best with what you have.

Write It Out

When you start comparing yourself with others, write down things to tell yourself to stop these thoughts in their tracks.

Example: "I have my own strengths. My tumbling has gotten so much better, and I am working on that new skill on beam that will increase the point value of my routine."

_____

_____

These comparisons with others might not end with bodies or gymnastics skills. You might even compare what you are eating. In college, on the way to practice every day I would eat a peanut butter and jelly sandwich. To me, this was a great source of energy before practice. It was the perfect combination of carbohydrates, protein, and sugar to get me through the next few hours. On top of being an energy source, it was also an easy and cheap meal: a win-win for a college student. One day I looked around to see what my teammates were eating. I saw someone eating a single granola bar, another person with a few slices of turkey and cheese, and then I noticed a teammate with...a *half* sandwich of peanut butter and jelly. One slice of bread with a little peanut butter and jelly. In that moment, I felt I was *obviously* eating too much. I then started having only half sandwiches as well. No one had said anything about what I was eating or how I looked, but in some ways, it felt like everyone was secretly competing to eat the least. Although I tried the half sandwich for some time, I did not lose weight. But my gymnastics (and my mood) were much worse.

Comparison can be a helpful motivator to improve your gymnastics or light a fire within yourself, but it should be used only for good. In this situation, it made me a worse gymnast, and I was denying my body the fuel it needed to perform its best and get stronger. Is comparison serving you? If not, then check out the preceding Write It Out sidebar, and brainstorm how to move beyond comparison and instead work to become the best version of yourself.

IN IT TOGETHER

Sometimes it can feel like you are going through an eating disorder very much alone, and sometimes it can feel like not eating is how you and others are bonding.

In the book *I'm Glad My Mom Died*, Jennette McCurdy, star of *iCarly* and *Sam & Cat*, describes how not eating and calorie counting was one way she and her mother bonded. They could share a salad (chicken and lettuce, with no dressing, obviously), and talk about how good (aka low) their calories were for the day. I have also seen this in gymnastics. When my teammate started developing an eating disorder, she and her roommate (who had an eating disorder) would bond over going to the workout center and spending hours on the cardio machines (this was on top of the previous five hours of practice and weights).

You are probably thinking how crazy this sounds. Unfortunately, it doesn't feel so crazy when your mind is telling you that you need to lose weight, you need to be smaller. Especially if you are close to someone with the same mindset, the excessive calorie counting and exercising can become normalized.

There would also be times after practice that the majority of the team would go to the workout center to get in just a bit more exercise. The previous five hours just weren't enough. Again, it didn't feel so crazy; it actually felt fun. We could all get thinner and fitter together. Especially if you start seeing results, it's an easy world to get sucked into.

HOW IT STARTS

Often, eating disorders start slow and then escalate quickly. My former teammate describes her experience: "It started pretty innocently. I was trying to eat lots of protein and not many carbohydrates." Her coaches noticed that she was losing weight, and for the most part, were very complimentary of her new, smaller figure and how fit she looked. She wasn't fit. She was skinny and it was a detriment to her gymnastics. Her mindset became, "Starve yourself and you'll get skinnier." One coach finally asked if she was okay because she was starting to wither away. My teammate explained that everything was fine, it was probably just the increased protein and decreased carbohydrates, nothing to be concerned about, although she was eating virtually no carbohydrates (aka fuel). She didn't have any energy. She described not being able to walk across campus without feeling exhausted. She couldn't concentrate in class. Her mind and body didn't have any carbohydrates to burn. She could even see her gymnastics performance declining, but the need to be skinny was more important than being good at gymnastics. Eventually, the loss of muscle led to a shoulder injury that required surgery. After surgery, the eating disorder worsened because she could eat even fewer calories without gaining weight compared with when she was training.

This story is one of many. Coaches, teammates, and even parents can often perpetuate these eating disorders by telling an athlete who has lost weight that they "look great," despite how the athlete feels internally. The preceding example involved an extreme reduction in caloric intake, or anorexia. Other athletes may turn to methods such as taking laxatives or diuretics to stay small or maintain a certain body fat percentage. Jennifer Sey, a former national team member and Olympic hopeful, described taking laxatives as a last resort in her memoir *Chalked Up: My Life in Elite Gymnastics*: "Just one year after having gone to Parkettes [a well-known gymnastics training center], one broken ankle, two black eyes, one eating disorder, untold boxes of laxatives, a few broken fingers, and splintered shins, I was the second-best gymnast in the country." This may sound extreme, but it is the reality for many gymnasts in these high-pressure environments.

ASK THE EXPERT: DR. LISA YOUNG

Dr. Lisa Young, RDN, PhD, is a registered dietitian, nutritionist, author, and adjunct professor at New York University. She shares her views on eating disorders and disordered eating, particularly for young athletes.

"It is important to get evaluated for an eating disorder and even for disordered eating as it affects both health and performance. Seeking both a therapist and nutritionist is crucial because if it goes unrecognized, it can lead to osteoporosis, amenorrhea, and a host of other problems. Additionally, it can lead to fatigue, weakness, and muscle loss, further affecting their performance. Early recognition and intervention are important in addressing eating disorders in young athletes to develop a healthier relationship with food and enhance their athletic performance."

Around the age of thirteen or fourteen, I remember purposely wearing my leotard before and after practice because it was so tight and would show any extra ounces of fat. This way, I would see exactly how my stomach looked in hopes that it would make me eat less. I always had teammates who were skinnier and more petite than myself. Everyone is built differently and I was built solid. I have strong legs and broad shoulders and in the gymnastics world, I was a "bigger girl." So my leotard tactic to be more conscious of what I was eating felt like a pretty good strategy to my young mind. As an adult, I can see how this was an extremely unhealthy mindset, but I've come to this understanding after years of positive self-talk. I now know that it is okay to look just as I do.

As one Stanford gymnast, Addie Stonecipher, stated in the *Stanford Daily*, "I don't think I've ever met a teammate who's had no issues with her body and didn't wish that anything was different, and I think that definitely says something about the nature of the sport."[56]

WHAT TO DO

Although extreme dieting culture and praise of being small hasn't completely disappeared from the world of gymnastics, the situation has certainly improved. If you are facing some sort of eating disorder or disordered eating, then the first thing to do is reach out for support. It could be a friend or family member. Even others who have been through similar experiences can be helpful, but speaking with a trained therapist can be life-changing.

Once you are working with a trained professional, they can help you with a treatment plan to figure out the triggers that cause the eating disorder or disordered eating. For some, this is not feeling good enough, stress (either in the gym or at home), not having the space to process emotions in a healthy way, worrying too much what others think, or a lack of control—to name a few.

In addition, you can work to reframe the way you look at and think about food. Instead of thinking of food as calories or either good or bad, think of food as fuel. Your body needs the best fuel to be able to do all the amazing things you do.

HEALTHY EATING

To be successful in this sport, it is essential to keep your body fueled. This keeps your energy up, promotes a better performance, helps prevent injury, and is better for your physical brain and mental health.

Not eating enough means that your body won't have the energy to train as you would like it to. It also means that you will be more likely to get injured and your body won't be able to repair itself as fast. Let's look at some of the main differences between healthy and disordered eating.

Healthy Eating	Disordered Eating
• Eating a variety of foods	• Limiting what you can eat
• Eating from all food groups	• Not eating certain food groups
• Eating on a regular schedule or when you're hungry	• Irregular eating (fasting and then bingeing, and so on)
• Being able to eat socially or attend social events that involve food	• Eating in secret or avoiding social gatherings that involve food
• Normal fluctuations in weight (1 to 4 pounds)	• Extreme fluctuations in weight (5 or more pounds)
• No guilt or shame with food	• Guilt or shame surrounding food

GETTING HELP

Reaching out for help is a great first step, but the perfect fit with a professional might not occur immediately. When my teammate eventually sought professional help, the first few people she met with always reverted back to calorie counting or her "healthy weight," insisting that she was consuming the "proper number of calories" or that she was "eating enough" for her body size. For her, this advice wasn't useful. She had been tracking calories in an attempt to manage her calories and weight for years. She needed to feel like a regular person again.

Eventually, she found a dietitian with a more holistic mindset. This dietitian insisted that she eat carbs and fats. And instead of counting calories or labeling food as good or bad, the dietitian asked her how different foods felt to her body. This helped shift her mindset to truly listen to her body.

CHANGING YOUR RELATIONSHIP WITH FOOD

The mindset of "good" versus "bad" food needs to change. The idea that you need to count calories or follow a math equation to be skinny also needs to change. Too many factors go into how much you should be eating: time spent training, type of training, time spent walking on campus, need for concentrating in class, and so on. Healthy eating means being in touch with your hunger and fullness cues, and everyone's body and needs are different. It is allowing your body to eat carbohydrates, fat, sugar—all demonized foods in society today. It is reflecting on how your body feels after eating to understand how to best fuel your unique body. When you practice healthy eating, you are more in tune with your body.

Learning the science of why your body needs all the different food groups is helpful. You need to eat carbs every three hours to keep your energy up. And protein, whole grains, and some fats are all healthy. Thinking about how your body is feeling after a meal or after you eat certain foods is much more useful than counting calories.

Even with all the knowledge in the world, you may still have a negative view of your body or a fear of gaining weight. As my former teammate shared, "Sometimes those negative thoughts and fears still creep in," even years after she has overcome her eating disorder. But now she listens to her body and can catch herself when these negative thoughts pop up. It is most important to correctly fuel your body to have energy and have the knowledge that everyone's caloric needs are different.

CHAPTER 9 KEY TAKEAWAYS

1. Body dysmorphia, eating disorders, and disordered eating are common in gymnastics due to the nature of the sport.

2. Not eating enough or eating in an irregular or disorderly way can lead to injuries, poor performance, mood swings, poor mental health, and formal eating disorders.

3. It is important to be aware of the differences between normal eating and disordered eating.

4. There is no such thing as the "perfect gymnast body." It is important to keep your body fueled to be at your best, both mentally and physically.

5. There are no such things as "good" or "bad" foods. Instead, focus on how you feel and your energy levels after eating certain foods. This is essential to performing your best and staying healthy.

PERFECTIONISM

"Perfect is the enemy of good."

—**Voltaire**

Gymnastics is a sport based on perfectionism, and because of this, it often breeds this characteristic in gymnasts. The premise of the sport is this: do everything perfectly and then get judged for how imperfect you are. It is difficult to find a gymnast who doesn't have some sort of perfectionist tendencies. You may not even be aware that you have these tendencies because they are so ingrained in your thought process. When I spoke with a former teammate, she shared how clear it is in gymnastics that you are always trying to be perfect; however, when you get out of the sport, you realize how much you crave being perfect in all other aspects of your life—the perfect student, daughter or son, friend, employee, with the perfect personality, body, career, and so on. Essentially, you want to carry around this perfect persona in and out of the gym.

WHAT IS PERFECTIONISM? WHAT IS PERFECT?

What is perfectionism? It is a personality trait where you are "striving for flaw-lessness and setting exceedingly high standards for performance, accompanied by tendencies for overly critical evaluations."[57] Because you train every day to execute perfect routines, it is easy to see how this leads to a perfectionist mindset. It is unlikely that you, or anyone you know, will ever do a perfect routine. Therefore you are stuck in an endless chase for the elusive perfect 10.

What is perfect? Trick question! There is no such thing as perfect. Perfection is relative. Just as beauty is in the eye of the beholder, so is perfection. You could do the exact same routine at two meets and get two completely different scores, simply because of who is judging you.

In this way, perfection can be whatever you want it to be. Create your own sense of perfect. When you are faced with a decision, think, "Is this perfect for *me*?" because true perfection doesn't exist.

PERFECTIONIST CHARACTERISTICS

Specific characteristics differentiate a perfectionist from someone who wants to get a job done, and done well. Perfectionists tend to be the following:

Highly self-critical: If you are always telling yourself that you need to be better, that you aren't doing enough even when you are doing your best, then you are being too critical. Rather than focusing on what you haven't done or haven't done well enough, take pride in everything you *have* accomplished.

Set unrealistic standards: Perfectionists often set standards for themselves that are unrealistic or unattainable. This creates unnecessary stress and pressure. Of course, you want to do the best routine you can, but don't see yourself as a failure because of a single wobble or mistake—or any number of wobbles or mistakes! It is unrealistic to do every routine perfectly every time. You are a human; give yourself some grace.

Seek instant success: Along with setting unrealistic standards, perfectionists often demand instant success. If you aren't successful immediately, then it feels like failure. But life isn't black and white, either perfection or failure; there is a gray area. If a skill isn't perfect the first time, then don't give up. Instead, keep practicing and you will gradually see improvement.

Have a strong fear of failure: Perfectionists fear failure, which can lead to procrastination, preventing perfectionists from moving forward. You may put off the task at hand because not trying at all is better than failing. Refer back to page 127 in chapter 8 on overcoming your fear of failure.

Results-obsessed: Perfectionists can be results-obsessed. This laser focus on results can sometimes be a good thing, but can also prevent you from seeing the bigger picture and alternative methods or routes to success. As much as possible, enjoy the process, not just the end result.

All-consuming: Perfectionists can become consumed by their lists, rules, and schedules, and how they come across to people. The need to accomplish, be perfect, see results, and so on, can take over your mind and use all your energy.

Perfectionism occurs because you want to do everything well (perfectly). But this often distracts you from getting anything accomplished. It is better to do something (which may or may not work out), rather than being frozen in fear that you won't be good enough. You may have heard the expression "Good is good enough." This means that nothing needs to be perfect; it just needs to get done.

When I talked with a former teammate, she explained how being perfect became an obsession in all aspects of her life. First, she wanted to have the perfect figure, so she would obsess about working out. But she also thought being perfect meant enjoying working out. So then she would obsess about enjoying the workout—a contradiction in itself. In addition, she had to have the perfect friends and perfect boyfriend, but she also had to get top grades. How exhausting! She didn't feel like herself because she was so focused on being the "perfect" version of herself in everyone else's eyes. In reality, just existing and being your true self is far healthier.

HOW IT STARTS

There are many ways the perfectionist mindset creeps in, particularly in the gym. Let's take a look at exactly how it starts.

CONTROL

A lot of perfectionism, like eating disorders (discussed in chapter 9), is rooted in control. In gymnastics, everything is in your control, but at the same time, nothing is in your control. You are the only one in charge of performing your routines, but also you can make mistakes and have no control over your score. You are the athlete but are also constantly told what to do, where you need to be, what you need to eat, what you need to look like, and so on. When so much is out of your control, it can feel like your own authority over your work, lists, rules, goals, and so on, is the only authority you have.

COMPARISON

Comparison is rampant in the gymnastics world. This is gymnasts comparing themselves with other gymnasts, coaches comparing athletes with other athletes, and sometimes even parents comparing their children with other team members. Comparison can drive perfectionism because you are constantly reminded of what others have achieved that you haven't. You may come to set your worth based on comparing yourself with others or their achievements.

Additionally, social media causes even more comparison with people we may not even know or ever interact with in person! It is too easy to compare yourself to unrealistic perfectionist ideals that you see on through edited Instagram, Snapchat, TikTok filters, or photoshopped in magazines or billboards. The people who you see online and compare yourself to probably don't even look like that in real life!

VALUE

Perfectionism can also begin from your value being based on your achievements, rather than your own sense of self-worth. If you feel the need to demonstrate great achievements in order to prove your worth, then you will feel a lot of pressure to be perfect. If you feel you will be loved only if you are perfect or reach a standard, then of course you will aim for perfection. But your value is so much more than your achievements, and you don't need to be anywhere close to perfect to be worthy. You are worthy because you exist.

THE DOWNHILL SLIDE

Wanting to do things perfectly can start with good intentions. You are focused on results and have set goals for yourself. But at a certain point, the focus on results becomes all you can think about. Your goals become unrealistic, and you have a nagging, constant fear of failure. This is the beginning of a downhill slide.

BURNOUT

One of the main dangers of perfectionism is that it can lead to burnout. Constantly trying to reach unattainable goals, particularly in a sport that is already so demanding, is exhausting and unsustainable. When you are physically working toward perfection on every event, day in and day out, and your mind is constantly telling you what you're doing is not good enough, this mindset takes both a physical and a mental toll on you.

HIDES YOUR TRUE SELF

Perfectionism also prevents you from being seen. Dr. Brené Brown, MSW, PhD, describes perfectionism as the ultimate fear. She says that "perfectionists walk around with a 20-ton shield because they are afraid that people will see them for who they really are."[58] You might think this shield will protect you from being hurt, but all it actually does is prevent people from knowing the real you.

HEALTH IMPLICATIONS

In addition to avoiding your true self, as well as feeling physically and mentally drained, perfectionism has also been shown to cause and perpetuate eating disorders, anxiety, and depression.[59] This aligns with the stress and obsessive tendencies that we talked about previously in this chapter. Some studies even show a higher risk of early mortality[60] when so much energy is spent on trying to prove something or reach unattainable goals.

Write It Out

Write down a time (either currently or in the past) when you were seeking perfection. As you remember this experience, answer the questions that follow:

- *Do I need to control this?*
- *What would not being perfect look like?*
- *What would change?*

_____

_____

_____

OVERCOMING PERFECTIONIST TENDENCIES

Although you will not transform your tendency toward perfectionism overnight, you can gradually unlearn or rethink your current mindset. Following are a few ideas to begin the process.

1. **Stop comparing yourself with others:** This is a great place to start. Look back on page 135 of chapter 9 to get some perspective on working with comparisons. All you can control is yourself. All you can do is your best.

2. **Set realistic standards:** It is great to have goals but keep them attainable.

3. **Alter your mindset:** There are some beneficial aspects of perfectionism. Alter your mindset from, "This has to be 100 percent perfect" to "This only has to be 75 percent or 50 percent perfect." This moves your thinking away from the extremes of either 100 percent failure or 100 percent perfection. There will never be something that you think is 100 percent perfect. When you set the level to 75 percent or 50 percent, that is still really good. And you can do so much more when things don't have to reach the level of total perfection.

   Also, with altering your mindset, think about what's going to change if you accept your lack of perfection. If you don't do a perfect routine, then you are still a great gymnast. If you don't have the perfect body, then you are still healthy and fit. If you don't throw the perfect birthday party, then everyone will still have a great time. Get some perspective.

4. **Don't sweat the small stuff:** This will take some time, but try to stay focused on the big picture. If you are working on a new floor routine, rather than trying to make every move perfect now, just get the choreography down and work on the flair later. It's not going anywhere. Or at a meet, instead of focusing on your hair and how it's not perfect, try to remember why you have a fancy hairstyle in the first place: to look and feel confident for the competition. Let yourself feel that confidence!

5. **Express yourself:** Find ways to express your thoughts. This could be writing. Speaking personally, writing this chapter has helped me immensely in understanding and coping with my perfectionism. You can also talk with friends, family, or a therapist. Sometimes the best way to get through something is to talk about it, to say the words aloud. Find what works for you to let go of unnecessary or unhelpful thoughts.

6. **Acceptance:** Although there are ways to help refocus and let go of perfectionism, some of these tendencies will never fully go away. You are human. Instead of trying to fully overcome being a perfectionist, start with a decrease in the number of times you think about the perfect outcome, situation, body image, and so on. Focus on this attainable goal, rather than trying to get rid of these thoughts completely. These thoughts will continue to reoccur in your life, so the focus should be on how you'll work through them, instead of how to stop them from happening. Be proud of your progress and direct your attention to decreasing the thing or thoughts that are negatively affecting you.

ARE YOU DOING THIS FOR OTHERS?

Why are you trying to be perfect? The answer is often to impress others or make others happy. In gymnastics, you may be trying to be perfect for your coach or your parents. It is easy to be so focused on the outcome that you don't know what is happening along the way. If your only goal is to impress others, then five years down the line you might realize that you don't actually want to do the sport or you don't love it, but you spent all that time and energy working just for the approval of others.

Additionally, we often think we need to do things to impress other people. We idealize other people and talk about how perfect their lives are. The truth is, everyone has their own troubles. That person who you think is so perfect may be going through the same troubles as you! You are trying your best and need to show compassion to yourself and those around you.

ASK THE EXPERT: DR. ALISON ARNOLD

Dr. Alison Arnold, MS, PhD (Doc Ali), shares her thoughts on overcoming and working with perfectionist tendencies.

"In order to overcome or work with perfectionist tendencies, it's important to know that self-compassion is essential to be your best. We are all human and make mistakes. You can acknowledge that you are human and make mistakes, while still seeing where you want to improve. It's all about balance.

"Gymnastics, in particular, walks a fine line in terms of being the best you can be and acknowledging your humanness. You can use improvement as motivation and still have compassion for yourself. It's so important to have both. It's great to constantly look to improve, but don't let it become an obsession. If your perfectionism causes you to shrink and feel self-hatred, that is when there is a problem and something to be looked at."

THE BENEFITS

Although we've spent a lot of time covering the negatives of perfectionism, there are some helpful aspects of holding yourself to this standard. For example, being the one who always does things correctly the first time is an invaluable skill. If you do the proper job (not necessarily the perfect job but a good job) every time, then you will be known as reliable and dependable. People know that if they entrust you with something, then it will be done and be done well. It also means that you pay attention to details, another important skill.

People with perfectionist tendencies also are often more motivated and focused than those without these tendencies. Your intense focus on doing the best job possible means you have the energy and endurance to continue to pursue a goal when others would give up. This level of motivation is not something that can be taught, so the fact that this comes naturally to you is very beneficial. You are a better worker, athlete, student, employee, and so on, with incredible staying power. You have greater motivation and a won't-give-up attitude, which is certainly a good thing—as long as it doesn't take over your life.

Although gymnastics might feel like your entire world right now, later it will feel like just a moment in time. Gymnastics does not need to define you, and neither should the need to be perfect. Your goal is to be your most present and authentic self, rather than constantly chasing perfection, which we know does not exist.

AFFIRMATIONS

Along with the methods already mentioned, another great way to shift your mindset is to repeat positive affirmations. Be aware of how you are talking to yourself so you can catch yourself when you become lost in a perfectionist mindset. Sharon Martin, LCSW, offers these affirmations for perfectionists.[61]

1. Progress over perfection.

2. Good enough really is good enough.

3. Perfection is unrealistic.

4. I don't have to do things perfectly.

5. Everyone makes mistakes.

6. I don't have to do it all.

7. It's healthy to relax and have fun.

8. Done is better than perfect.

9. Enjoy the process, not just the outcome.

10. My worth isn't based on my achievements.

CHAPTER 10 KEY TAKEAWAYS

1. Gymnastics breeds perfectionism because the premise of the sport is to be as close to perfection as possible.

2. Perfectionism means setting unrealistic standards of achievement and being overly self-critical.

3. A lot of perfectionism comes from comparing yourself with others, including teammates, friends, and other athletes, as well as comparing yourself with unrealistic perfectionist ideals (that is, Instagram photos, photoshopped magazine photos, and so on). Perfectionism can also come from thinking your value lies in your achievements, rather than believing in your own inherent worth.

4. Perfectionism can lead to burnout, in addition to physical and mental issues.

5. Overcoming and working through perfectionist tendencies first means realizing that there is no such thing as perfect; it is all in the eye of the beholder. Then you must catch yourself when you have these thoughts and replace them with a positive affirmation. This way, you can be your most authentic self.

CHAPTER 11

INJURIES

"Being challenged is inevitable. Being defeated is optional."

—Anonymous

An unfortunate but inevitable part of gymnastics, and sports in general, is injuries. As much as you try to eat well, take care of your body, sleep enough, do prehabilitation, stretch, and so on, injuries still occur. Gymnastics has the unfortunate distinction of having one of the highest injury rates among girls' sports[62] with similar injury rates among boys and girls.[63]

In this chapter, we will discuss the most common injuries in the sport, how injuries occur, ways to prevent injuries, and how to overcome injuries.

THE ORDINARINESS OF INJURIES

Although injuries are bound to happen in any sport, there are a few reasons why gymnasts are particularly susceptible to them. The first is the long practice hours. Long hours can lead to overuse injuries, such as tendinitis, stress fractures, growth plate injuries, and so on. Long hours can also lead to both mental and physical fatigue, which can mean an increased chance of hurting yourself. This could be landing short, incorrect timing, stepping off a mat incorrectly, or even tripping. As silly as it sounds, some of the worst injuries I've seen (some even requiring surgery) were caused by jumping on a block or stepping off equipment just slightly wrong. You do incredibly dangerous and challenging tricks daily, but sometimes it's one fluke turn or step that takes you out the longest.

Gymnastics also requires a great deal of repetition in order to create muscle memory and refine your skills. Most skills require putting considerable force on upper extremities, particularly wrists, elbows, and shoulders. In the lower body, you are constantly pounding your knees, hips, ankles, back, and so on. Doing the same thing repeatedly and putting constant force on your joints can lead to long-term injuries or chronic pain.

In addition to the long hours and repetitive movements, gymnastics is a year-round sport. This means that there isn't much time for your body to recover. Taking time off is usually viewed negatively for your skill progression and fitness, and fears might appear once you are back in the gym. Because of this, you might take time off only when you are forced to due to an injury.

Unlike some sports, gymnastics is a full-body sport, leaving opportunities for both lower body and upper body injuries. For example, soccer mainly causes lower body injuries and swimming mainly causes upper body injuries because in those two sports, the required movement is either focused on the lower body or the upper body. In gymnastics, because you are on your hands as much as you are on your feet, the full body is fair game.

Finally, gymnastics skills are complicated and highly technical. When skills are not performed correctly, or with accurate cues and timing, it is easy to miss a hand, foot, or landing, leading to serious injury. During competition, with the help of adrenaline, you might flip higher or move faster—and there might be fewer mats and a lack of your usual visual cues. All these factors can increase your likelihood of injury.

COMMON INJURIES

Due to the variety of skills in gymnastics, there is a wide range of possible injuries. It is common for men to have more upper body injuries because most events are focused on the upper body, while women tend to have more ankle and foot injuries.[64] Common injuries across the board are wrist and ankle sprains, shoulder or elbow dislocation, back injuries, Achilles tendon tears, and anterior cruciate ligament (ACL) tears, to name a few. In addition to the skills you are training, certain factors can add to your risk of injury.

FLEXIBILITY

Flexibility is integral to success in gymnastics, and therefore time is dedicated every day to stretching. Most coaches know that if their athletes don't stretch enough before or after practice, they are more likely to get hurt. Stretching ensures your muscles are loose, warm, and active, and allows your body to move and bend in the planned or unplanned positions of gymnastics skills. Flexibility also improves your range of motion, which means you are less likely to over-stretch and pull or strain a muscle.

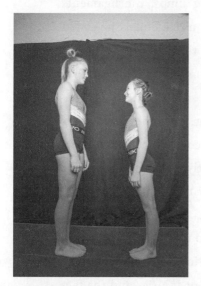

On the other hand, being too flexible can also make you more susceptible to injury. When there is excess elasticity, particularly in your knees, hips, or shoulders, your muscles can easily push beyond the normal range of motion limit. One of my college teammates had beautiful lines because her knees could naturally hyperextend. Even when her legs weren't straight, she still had a perfectly straight handstand line. Check out the picture that follows to get an idea. Although it made her gymnastics look beautiful, it also meant that if she landed too forcefully or slightly twisted, her knees couldn't handle it. She had four knee surgeries before the age of twenty.

It's helpful to have hyperextending knees for beautiful handstands, but in my teammate's case, it also led to increased injuries. It was too easy for her knees to bend too much the wrong way, especially when there was added force from a landing or fall.

I know, sometimes it feels like you can't win; you need to be flexible but also can't be too flexible. It may feel like no matter what you do, you can get hurt. Both poor flexibility and hyper-flexibility are extremes, but it's important to be aware of both the benefits and the drawbacks of flexibility.

POSITIVE ENDING

My teammate with the hyperextended knees (along with hyperextended elbows) is a true testament to perseverance. Her freshman year of high school, she tore her ACL and had to have surgery. When she was almost recovered from the injury and was starting to come back, she tore it again on a simple leap. She had to have another surgery. This time, part of her hamstring was moved to her ACL.

In addition to her hyperextending limbs, the ligaments connected to her kneecaps were also quite mobile. She ended up dislocating her kneecaps multiple times, until she had to have surgery to replace the loose tendons with thicker patellar tendons to keep her kneecaps secure.

After all this, you may be hoping for some good news. Unfortunately, in her junior year of college she took a turn where she landed with her knee slightly twisted. She tore her ACL, medial collateral ligament (MCL), and lateral collateral ligament (LCL). At this point she was ready to throw in the towel and quit gymnastics. She was so tired of going through pain, surgery, rehabilitation, and getting back in shape. She felt mentally drained from her constant injuries and the fact that she had to be at practice every day without being able to do anything or contribute to the team.

In the end, she decided that because she had only one more year of college gymnastics, she would stick with it. It didn't make her comeback easier though. She had to switch her mindset from focusing on everything that she couldn't do to focusing on "What is my role now?" Because she wasn't able to practice, she could be a helpful teammate by moving mats, assisting with choreography, or mentoring those who were struggling.

After her final, grueling recovery process, it was her senior year. She stayed focused on maintaining her health and fitness and always prioritized prehabilitation exercises to prevent injury as much as she could. She competed bars in every meet in her last year and had a fantastic senior season.

It took a while to build up the strength in her knees again, but today she has no knee pain, despite running numerous half-marathons, consistently lifting weights, skiing, hiking, and so on. I hope this story is an inspiration: despite hardships, you can overcome whatever injury you face.

AGE

Just as you can't make your knees less flexible, you can't change the fact that you are getting older. Age also has an effect on your likelihood of injury. As you get older, there are a few reasons there is more potential for injury. First, with age (usually) comes more hours spent training. Increased time in practice provides more opportunity for injury to occur. Second, as you get older, you progress in levels, skills, and the difficulty of the skills. When skills are more challenging, accurate timing is even more critical. The more difficult skills also require more time in the air to complete the movement, so you need to be aware of more cues and corrections. Practicing more challenging skills, which require precise timing, while also doing higher flips are all added ways to hurt yourself.

Additionally, as you get older, you grow! You are now moving longer limbs and more weight. Not only is your timing different, but also more force is being exerted on your joints, muscles, and entire body. Although growing is a wonderful thing, it leads to its own set of issues in gym, as we will discuss in the next two sections.

GROWING PAINS

For girls, the most significant growth period is between ages nine and fourteen, and for boys it is between ages eleven and sixteen.[65] Growth is expected and a positive thing, but sometimes it doesn't feel so great for your body. Intense training coinciding with rapid growth can cause pain, particularly at the growth plates, such as the knees, heels, and shoulders.

The common growth-related pain at the knees is called Osgood-Schlatter's disease, which is inflammation in the knee (or to be specific, the tibial tuberosity).[66] When I was growing, I had heel pain, called Sever's disease, which is inflammation of the growth plate in the heel.

In addition to pain being uncomfortable and frustrating, the primary cure for growth plate–related injuries is to rest and allow the area to finish growing (which is even more frustrating because taking time off usually isn't an option!). Stretches and strengthening exercises can be helpful, along with ice and sometimes heel or knee cushions or braces.

In addition to pain at your growth areas, growing also changes your spatial awareness, which can really throw you off.

GROWING FRUSTRATION

It may have taken awhile, but all the skills you have, you learned when you were a particular size; however, adolescence causes a sharp rate of growth. You were also familiar with your timing and where to spot. But now that you have to move much longer limbs, your timing is off and your visual cues are different; nothing feels right. You may have lost a skill or skills that once were so easy. It can be an extremely distressing time because your body, cues, balance, and how you are used to moving have all changed.

Even though I'm not particularly tall (at five feet three), I grew much taller than some of my other teammates, who finished growing at four feet ten. It was disconcerting because I lost skills and saw a slowdown in my skill progression during this time due to my new body. And I felt less coordinated than ever before because of these changes. Also, although coaches may be aware of the changes you're going through, they often expect the same results. This can feel discouraging because you (and your coach) can't understand why things that used to be easy aren't so easy anymore.

To make matters worse, your peak growth is also the time when you are more likely to get injured. During growth spurts, your bone density temporarily decreases, as do coordination and spatial awareness. This combination of factors is the perfect recipe for injury. Although you can't change what's happening with your body, knowing what is happening and that it is normal should help you remember that you're not suddenly bad at gymnastics. You and your mind simply must get used to your new body, and it will take some time.

PREVENTING INJURY

Although sometimes injuries are out of your control, there are plenty of things you can do to help yourself avoid them. Take particular care at this age to fuel and rest your body. Answer the questions that follow to determine if you are keeping yourself in peak performance mode.

ARE YOU EATING ENOUGH?

Often we don't think about how much we're eating, and instead think about just avoiding "the bad foods." But adequate nutrition has a huge effect on how your body recovers after practice. Sometimes the need to be what we consider fit is so strong that we limit what we eat in order to accomplish this, not thinking about the consequences for the body.

Being fit means you are giving yourself enough food to maintain and strengthen your muscles. You can't be fit if you aren't able to finish your routines!

If you aren't giving your body enough calories, then you aren't providing your body with sufficient energy. Low energy also means you are more tired and unfocused, both of which can lead to injury. For example, if you haven't eaten enough food to fuel your body, then you will feel exhausted at the end of your floor routine. This may cause you to land a pass short and injure a knee or an ankle. Also, your muscles need food to rebuild and repair themselves after a long day of practice. Not enough food in your body means there isn't enough food for your muscles to repair themselves. And not allowing your muscles to recover means that any minor strains could become bigger injuries. It is also much more difficult for your body to grow muscle if it doesn't have fuel due to a lack of calories. As we talked about in chapter 2, having and maintaining muscle is beneficial for injury prevention.

HOW IS YOUR DIET?

Along with eating enough food, eating the right food is also extremely important. A balanced, nutrient-rich diet is important for athletes to fuel their bodies and ensure optimal performance. What are the right foods? According to Dr. Lisa Young, RDN, PhD, registered dietitian, nutritionist, author, and adjunct professor at New York University, a balanced, nutrient-rich diet is "a variety of fruits, vegetables, whole grains, nuts, seeds and legumes." These foods provide essential vitamins, minerals, antioxidants, and fiber for overall health, to support immune function, and to reduce inflammation. Dr. Young adds that "healthy fats, such as olive oil, fatty fish, and avocados, provide an energy source and help your body to absorb certain fat-soluble vitamins."

ARE YOU HYDRATED?

Along with eating well and eating enough, staying hydrated is crucial to prevent injuries. This doesn't mean hydrating just during practice; it means hydrating throughout the day, every day. Make sure you are staying consistently hydrated to feel better, help with your concentration, keep your muscles loose, move nutrients around your body, and increase your endurance. The more hydrated your body, the less likely you are to tear a muscle or tendon.

ARE YOU GETTING ENOUGH SLEEP?

Sleep is also a critical factor to staying healthy and injury-free. Getting enough sleep means 9 to 12 hours for ages six to twelve. And it means 8 to 10 hours for those age thirteen to eighteen. As you get older, you don't need as much sleep, but even adults should be getting seven hours at a minimum. In addition to how much you are sleeping, the quality of your sleep is important. If your sleep is interrupted or your room is too bright, then this can affect your sleep quality. Looking at your phone or other electronics before bed also affects your sleep because of the screen light and the fact that you're revving up your mind, which makes it harder to fall asleep. You need a long, uninterrupted sleep to perform at your best.

Sleep and rest allow your body to recover and provide energy for the following day. Sleep also influences your speed and reaction time. Having a quicker reaction time could be the difference between getting hurt and staying free from injury.

HOW IS YOUR WARM-UP?

Sometimes warming up feels like a chore. You do it every day, and it can become monotonous. But those 30 minutes or so warming up, and warming up properly, are imperative for injury avoidance. If you are just going through the motions during warm-up, then you are doing yourself a disservice. While you warm up, focus on what muscles you are stretching, and think about loosening your joints and priming your body for the intense workout that you are about to do. If you aren't getting your muscles, joints, and mind warmed up, then your body won't be ready for all the crazy flips and twists that it's about to do.

If you are intentional and focused during your warm-up, you may notice areas of your body that are tight. This is a great time to spend a few extra minutes focusing on these specific areas.

As we discussed in chapter 4, the coordination of gymnastics is all about different muscle groups working together. If one muscle group isn't warmed up but is forced to work by another muscle group, then this could also lead to injury.

HOW IS YOUR STRENGTH?

As noted in chapter 2, being stronger helps prevent injuries. That's why it's important to put in your best effort during conditioning. Think back on that mind-body connection we talked about in chapter 4. If you are really focused on the muscle groups you are using and what skills or events you'll use those muscle groups for, then that can really help. Work hard during conditioning. Your body will thank you later, when it can protect itself after a weird fall!

It's also important to know whether you have any strength imbalances. For example, when I first learned how to lift weights in college, my leg strength improved significantly in a short time. Although my legs were stronger, I wasn't spending the same amount of time strengthening my core. This created a significant strength imbalance; my legs (specifically my hamstrings) were much stronger than my core, which caused an uneven pulling on my back, leading to pain. To get rid of my back pain, I had to focus on strengthening my back and core, thus balancing everything out.

HOW DOES YOUR TECHNIQUE LOOK?

In addition to everything already mentioned, your technique, or how you execute your skills, has a major influence on your odds of injury. Practicing with an incorrect technique can put unnecessary strain on certain muscles or body parts, which could lead to injury. For example, if you aren't squeezing your core, and your back and shoulders are loose during a handstand, this constant incorrect movement can eventually lead to back pain or injury. To get a visual, check out

Incorrect technique   Correct technique

the photo of the correct versus incorrect technique, which follows. Additionally, if you aren't focused on the correct technique and are loose during a skill, then this leaves room for error and you could possibly fall and injure yourself.

The technique shown on the left with bad (loose) form puts significantly more pressure on the lower back. Additionally, the technique on the left is much less stable than the proper form of the handstand on the right, thus increasing the likelihood of falling.

WHAT IS YOUR MINDSET?

After focusing on what your body is doing, take a minute to focus on your thoughts. If your mind is full of negativity or stress, then this can increase inflammation. And inflammation can make minor injuries worse and prevent current injuries from healing. In addition, research has shown that depression or anxiety can increase your risk of injury.[67] Not being in the right headspace can distract you from what is going on, also increasing your risk of injury. Stay aware of your mindset because it influences how you act, react, and perform.

Is your mind filled with fear? When you are fearful, you might not move as confidently or powerfully as you should, affecting how you complete the skill. If aren't fully confident about doing a skill by yourself, then make sure to get a spot or use soft mats—or both—until you are able to perform the skill properly.

ARE YOU COMMUNICATING?

In addition to what you are telling yourself, communicating with your coaches is crucial for preventing injury. There is no need to fret about every minor ache or pain, but if you have constant, serious pain, then you should communicate with your coach or seek medical advice. It could be nothing or it could lead to a worse injury. It is best to find out sooner rather than hurting yourself more later.

Specific braces or equipment can mitigate and improve chronic pain. For example, I have very inflexible wrists, and wearing wrist supports (also known as Tiger Paws) made a massive difference for me. There are braces and pads for the feet, ankles, knees, elbows, back, and so on, which can make your life so much better.

Daniel Miranda, cofounder, CEO, and head coach of Gotham Gymnastics (Brooklyn, New York), shares how his team works to prevent injuries as much as possible.

"Every day we have all the gymnasts complete a daily assessment, which asks a set of questions about their sleep, mood, stress, fatigue, soreness. The assessment also has a body chart where the athlete can pinpoint areas that are in pain or tight. When I see specifically where they are hurt or sore, I can make sure not to push that area or body part. We also do a jump test and compare it to the gymnast's normal jump height to see if their body is functioning normally or not. This helps to avoid extremely serious injuries that could take a gymnast out for an extended period of time."

FACING INJURY

So you've done everything you can to prevent injury, but you've still gotten hurt. What's next? Well, there are a few things to start with.

RICE

If an injury occurs, then the first thing you might hear your coach say is "RICE." This is an acronym for a method to treat injuries until you get a diagnosis from a medical professional.

- **Rest:** Stay off the injured area and avoid putting any weight on the area.
- **Ice:** Hold ice on the area to reduce pain and swelling.
- **Compression:** Bandage the area firmly but not too tightly (too tight can interfere with blood flow).

- **Elevation:** Keep the injured area above the level of your heart. For example, if you hurt your ankle, then sit or lie down with your foot elevated. This will also help reduce swelling.

The RICE method helps reduce immediate damage, inflammation, and pain, and it kick-starts the healing process.

ICE AND HEAT

RICE is an easy method to remember and is a great first step for treating any injury. After the acute injury, consistent use of plain old ice or heat can be highly beneficial, depending on the injury.

If you have swelling, bruising, or inflammation, then ice helps reduce these symptoms. For example, after I sprained my ankle, I would put my foot in a bucket of ice water every day for 10 to 15 minutes (after the first 5 minutes, your foot goes numb) to reduce the swelling and bruising. Other injuries for which it's helpful to use ice are tendinitis or growing pains because ice helps numb the area. Ice can also be used to reduce bone or joint pain.

Ice should not be placed directly on your skin. Wrap the ice in a paper towel or cloth, because holding ice directly on the skin for an extended period of time can cause ice burns. Ice buckets or ice baths are different because they are just very cold water and do not require you to place ice on your skin.

Heat, on the other hand, brings blood to the area, which is why it shouldn't be applied for the first 48 hours after an injury. Heat helps reduce stiffness in muscles, and it helps increase your range of motion. You can also warm up your muscles using heat.

Knowing how best to treat your injuries is important to encourage healing as fast as possible.

GET STRONGER

The next part of dealing with an injury is refocusing your mind to stop looking at what you can't do because of your injury and instead focus on what you can do. Why not spend some of the extra time you have on getting stronger? For example, with a wrist injury you can focus on getting your lower body and core strong. With a lower body injury, you can get your upper body and core strong. Having a strong core will help with just about every skill in gymnastics and will help prevent one of the most common sources of discomfort and pain: back injuries.

In addition to doing conditioning exercises, focus on the parts of your routines that you can still train. For example, if you have an upper body injury, then you won't be doing bars, but you can do lots of running drills to improve your speed and ultimately your vault. Or do lots of dance throughs on the floor to make your choreography flawless. You don't usually get to spend so much time on these things, but now you can!

STRETCH

While getting stronger during an injury, you can also work on getting more flexible. Again, when do you normally have the time to dedicate an hour to stretching? This is your chance! You can improve not only your split flexibility, but also your shoulders, hip flexors, toe point, wrists, and so on.

MINDSET

With the extra time you have now, you can also spend some time improving your mindset. You can feel sorry for yourself for being hurt. Or you can have the mindset of someone who overcomes any obstacle thrown their way. It is your choice.

In addition to a victorious mindset, you can also build up your mental training. This is the perfect time to get your mental training up to the level of your physical training. Mental training involves thinking (or saying) your verbal cues and imagining (or physically) tightening the muscles that need to be tightened. This will have a profound effect on how fast you return from an injury.

I was lucky and had only a few injuries throughout my 16-year career. What I hated most about being hurt was having to go to practice every day and seeing my teammates getting better, while I sat back and watched. Although it is important to stay fit and do conditioning while hurt, it still stings being in the gym and not getting to train your skills. If you've ever felt like this, then remember it is important to stay connected with your teammates and coaches. They can keep you in touch with what is going on and encourage you to get back as soon as possible. Everyone gets hurt at some point, so they know how difficult it is to be in your shoes. If you are struggling, then ask a teammate who recently came back from an injury how they dealt with it and if they have any tips to stay fit physically and stay strong and positive mentally.

ENJOY SOME DOWNTIME

Injuries can even be good fortune in disguise. Do you remember that we talked about how so much time is dedicated to training, with no time off? Well, here you are with this dedicated time that you must take off. The time off can help repair other body parts that have been in pain, overused, or close to the point of injury.

You can also use this time to do things that you normally don't have time for. Maybe it's going to a sporting event at school or spending time with other friends. Time with an injury will go by much faster if you are spending that time on things that you enjoy doing! Appreciate this brief vacation while you have it.

REHABILITATION

At long last, you are reaching the end of your injury. Doing rehabilitation exercises will help you get back to practice as soon as possible. These exercises strengthen both the injured part as well as the surrounding muscles so you can regain your range of motion.

Rehabilitation exercises vary according to which body part was injured. They can include everything from swimming rehabilitation to physical therapy exercises to the use of resistance bands or light weights at home. Some examples of exercises follow.

Ankle rehab exercise

Ankle injury: The photo to the right shows a great rehabilitation exercise for any ankle injury. Place the resistance band on the ball of your foot (as shown), and point and flex your foot with the band as resistance. Do this 25 times and then switch feet.

In addition to moving your foot up and down, you can also move it from side to side, again with the band as resistance. Do this exercise 25 times on each foot, and see how strong and resilient your ankles become!

Hip stability and strength: The exercise on the right is helpful for hip stability and strength.

Place the resistance band on the middles of your shins (as shown). Lift your leg until you feel resistance and then lower it. Do this 10 to 15 times on both sides. Make sure to maintain at least some resistance in the band when you lower the leg to avoid the band falling down your leg.

Exercise for hip stability and strength

Shoulder rehabilitation and strengthening: The exercise shown on the right is beneficial for shoulder rehabilitation and strengthening.

Place the resistance band on your wrists, and pull your hands apart as far as they can go. Repeat this 10 to 20 times until you feel it. This is a simple exercise that you can do every day to warm up and strengthen your shoulders and upper body.

Exercise for shoulder rehab and strengthening

THE DISCOURAGEMENT

There is no good time to get injured, but as you know, the worst times are right before the season starts or before that big competition. Maybe you even just came back from an injury, and then you got hurt again. It is incredibly frustrating and discouraging. Sometimes it feels like you can't catch a break. No matter what you do, your body always finds a way to get hurt. You may want to quit gymnastics altogether because of injuries and feeling like you are always hurt. There are a few reasons you may be feeling so discouraged.

COMMUNITY

First, so much of the joy of gymnastics comes from spending time with your teammates and friends. When you can't train as usual, you are missing that sense of community, which is so powerful, particularly at this age. You probably also feel FOMO (fear of missing out) because you don't get to spend time with your friends in the same way you usually do. Although it is not easy, remaining a supportive teammate is the best way to maintain your connections and community.

PURPOSE AND IDENTITY

Another reason injuries are frustrating is that when you're not training or pursuing your goals, it can feel like you've lost your sense of purpose. When your identity is tied to being a gymnast, if you are unable to train, then it also feels like you are losing your identity. If anything, then your injury should remind you how much of an athlete you actually are. Injuries are part of any sport. You have the ability to define the narrative of what happens after your current setback. Use that as fuel to keep pursuing your purpose and goals, despite your current constraints.

MOTIVATION

It is not easy to stay motivated or want to continue with the sport when you are injured. Know that what you are feeling is normal and will not last forever. To stay motivated, focus on the things that are within your control (mindset, being a good teammate, strength, and flexibility); how you can best recover (rehabilitation); and mental training to keep your body and mindset strong.

THE COMEBACK

Once you are cleared by your medical provider, you're probably raring to get back into the gym and jump back to where you were. But that may be asking to get hurt again. Make sure you come back in slowly and with baby steps. You don't want to rush back and reinjure yourself. And you definitely don't want to sustain a new injury by jumping back in too soon. Your muscles need to build back to training level. Easing back into training is just another phase in coming back; don't try to skip or rush through this important time.

PHYSICAL RECOVERY

It's important not to push yourself too much, too soon when you return. This can further delay your recovery and possibly cause you to reinjure yourself. Listen to your body. Getting all your skills back will be a gradual process. Remember the benefits of having that time off: giving your body some good rest and strengthening and stretching areas of your body that you wouldn't normally focus on. Take your comeback one day at a time. Injuries only make you that much stronger, mentally and physically. You have overcome your injury and made it to the other side. Make sure you listen to your body. Take it easy when something hurts.

MENTAL RECOVERY

Something that can be just as powerful as the physical healing of your body is the mental recovery. Encourage your physical comeback by having a positive mindset and using your mind to visualize. Research has shown that envisioning mental imagery of your routines and skills is beneficial to prevent the strength loss that occurs during injury (from disuse), which means you can come back sooner.[68]

ASK THE EXPERT: DR. LISA YOUNG

Certain foods are helpful in your recovery process. Dr. Lisa Young, RDN, PhD, says that "lean protein, such as fish, poultry, legumes, and dairy products, is essential for muscle repair and recovery. While you should be eating lean protein all the time (since your muscles are constantly being worn down by working out and need to recover), this is even more essential when you have a muscular tear injury. You want to help your body repair itself as fast as possible to get you back on track.

"Zinc-rich foods have been shown to aid in recovery and support the body's healing processes, since they promote tissue repair and regeneration, [encourage] collagen production, and improve immune function. Examples of zinc-rich foods include nuts, seeds, whole grains, legumes, and lean meats.

"Other foods high in protein, vitamin C, vitamin D, and antioxidants can help with tissue repair, muscle recovery, and optimal healing. Dairy products also contribute to bone health as they are rich in calcium and vitamin D. Other good sources to promote strong bones include nuts, seeds, fish, leafy green vegetables, and legumes."

All this is to say, injuries will always be part of gymnastics, as they are in any sport. And as the anonymous quote at the beginning of the chapter points out, challenges, such as injury, are inevitable. How you face these challenges—whether you succumb to them or overcome them—is up to you.

CHAPTER 11 KEY TAKEAWAYS

1. Injuries are common in gymnastics due to the long training hours, repetitive movements, lack of time off, and difficult skills.

2. Growth spurts are normal but increase the likelihood of injuries and can throw off your timing, which can lead to frustration.

3. These are steps you can take to help keep your body healthy and avoid injuries: consume enough food, consume healthful foods, stay hydrated, sleep at least eight hours a night, do a good warm-up, maintain strength, have good technique, maintain a positive mindset, and communicate with your coaches.

4. When an injury first occurs, remember RICE (rest, ice, compression, elevation). After the initial injury, use ice, heat, strengthening exercises, stretching, a good mindset, enjoyment of the downtime, and rehabilitation to get you through.

5. Overcoming injuries requires a combination of both physical and mental recovery techniques, as well as feeling supported.

***

You have made it through parts 1 and 2! I hope you can see all aspects of the sport and are ready to think about your next steps. Do you want to continue pursing gymnastics and earn a college scholarship? Or have you reached the end of your road and want to look for alternatives to the sport? We will get into all of that and more in part 3.

PART III

MAKING A DECISION

QUITTING

Now that we have explored the best and worst parts of gymnastics, it is time to weigh your options and come to a decision. My hope is that whatever decision you make, you now have all the necessary information and can make your decision confidently. If you are leaning toward staying in gymnastics, then check out page 186, where ways to earn a gymnastics college scholarship are covered. If you are still on the fence or leaning toward quitting, then keep reading. There are still some other options...

TAKE A STEP BACK

Gymnastics asks a lot of you, especially at such a young age. It is difficult to decide if this is what you want to continue dedicating so much of your time and energy to, or even whether this is what you'd like to do for another four years in college. That's a lot of pressure! It doesn't have to be that way.

BE PRESENT

Instead of wondering how you'll feel at the end of the year or even at the end of your junior or senior year of high school, think about only today. About this moment. Are you looking forward to practice? Are there any skills that you are excited about? A friend that you can't wait to spend time with? Really reflect on what makes you want or not want to go to the gym. You don't need to figure everything out right now! If there are still things you enjoy about gymnastics, then you don't need to make any big decisions right away.

GAMIFY

Work with your coach to alter assignments or conditioning to make practice more enjoyable. As you know, sometimes practice can feel repetitive. You can change this. See how many routines you can stick into a game. Or how many handstands you can hit as a team. Switching things up and creating individual or team games can help show you that this is *just gymnastics*. It doesn't have to always be so serious! It can *and should be* fun! This may also help you look forward to practice and enjoy your time there.

TAKE THE PRESSURE OFF

Another reason for not liking gymnastics anymore is feeling too much pressure. This could be pressure you are putting on yourself. Or it could be pressure from your parents, coaches, and so on. Maybe you feel pressure to move up levels too quickly or learn skills that you don't feel ready for. Identify where this stress is coming from. Often it is something that can be changed. For example, if you feel rushed to move up levels or learn too many new skills, then one option is to repeat a level. I repeated levels 8, 9, and 10. Taking the time to master those levels not only gave me confidence, but also allowed me to prepare for my next level while competing at a lower level. This increased the amount of time I had to prepare for the next level, so it wasn't such a stressful transition.

If staying at your current level is still too much, then you can move down a level. If you make this choice, then it doesn't change anything about how good a gymnast you are. Rather, it allows you to fall back in love with the sport without the stress of constantly learning more and more challenging skills.

Write It Out

On a separate piece of paper, try making a pro and con list of what you love and don't love about the gym to help process the many thoughts going through your mind. Try as best as you can to be objective, and write out everything that pops into your head.

TAKE A BREATHER

Finally, if you've tried all the preceding ideas and are still frustrated with gym, then give yourself a break. This could mean taking time off so you have the space to reflect. You don't get much downtime in gymnastics, so create it yourself. Allow yourself time to process all your thoughts.

Taking time off is a great way to see what it would feel like to not have gymnastics in your life. During the break you might realize that you can't live without gymnastics—or you might not miss it at all.

If you've tried all these ideas and still aren't convinced one way or the other, then I have some gym alternatives for you.

ALTERNATIVES

If your heart isn't in competitive gymnastics, also known as development track, then there are alternatives. You could remain in the sport with less intensity. There are other programs around the country where you can still compete and perform with some nuance. First, there is Xcel, which is still competitive but more flexible than the development track. It is also less of a time commitment for those who want to pursue other sports at the same time. Unlike development track, Xcel does not require you to compete in all four events, so you can focus on the events that you enjoy most. There are still "levels" in Xcel, which roughly align with development track. See the following:

Xcel	Development Track
Bronze	Levels 1–2
Silver	Level 3
Gold	Level 4–5
Platinum	Level 5–6
Diamond	Level 6–7
Sapphire	Level 8–10

Xcel allows you to continue to compete and achieve as an athlete, but without some of the things you don't enjoy that are part of the development track.

If your gym doesn't offer Xcel, then there are some local leagues that are similar to Xcel. For example, in Maryland, Virginia, and Pennsylvania, there is Mason Dixon; in Texas, there is the Texas Amateur Athletic Federation (TAAF); and in New Jersey, there is the Jersey Optional Gymnastics Association (JOGA). These alternatives to the development or JO track allow athletes to still experience competitive gymnastics, just in a less intense environment that allows for more experiences outside the gym.

WHEN QUITTING IS OKAY

Growing up, we're always told to never give up and never quit. US football coach Vince Lombardi said, "Quitters never win and winners never quit." Don't get me wrong: there is certainly growth that can come through sticking with something despite its challenges and disappointments. But when you get to your breaking point because you have long-term injuries that will be a detriment for the rest of your life; you have malicious coaches, teammates, or trainers; you dislike the extreme time commitment; or the sport is simply not fun anymore, then quitting may be the correct choice for you.

I recently listened to an interview with University of Chicago economics professor Dr. John List, PhD. He talked about the strong emphasis our society puts on "not being a quitter." Although there are fantastic stories about people who pursued their goals despite severe obstacles and never gave up, List notes that it is sometimes okay to move on to something else where you may have strengths that you were not able to pursue previously. He cited his personal example of being a very talented golfer in middle school and high school. He earned a college scholarship and had plans to become a professional golfer. But after looking at his scores compared with those of people he was competing against, he realized that he was simply not up to their level. Although it certainly wasn't an easy decision, he was able to let go of golf and eventually found another talent: researching and teaching economics. This is now his life passion, and he has been published more than 250 times and has won countless awards.[69]

If you are staying in the sport only to avoid disappointing your parents or coaches, then realize that you are the one who is putting in the time, work, and energy, and you should be the one making the decision about what is best for you. If you don't want to quit only because you will miss your friends, then that is also not a good reason to stay in the sport. You will still get to see your friends outside the gym, and if that is the only reason you are going to practice, then you are not doing the sport for yourself.

ASK THE EXPERT: DANIEL MIRANDA

Daniel Miranda, cofounder, CEO, and head coach of Gotham Gymnastics (Brooklyn, New York) shares his thoughts about determining whether you should quit gymnastics.

"After you have recovered from anything you are going through, whether it's an injury, stress, anxiety, fear, etc., when you are feeling good about yourself is when you should decide whether or not to quit. You should only make a decision when you are up and feeling confident about yourself. If you decide on your best, happiest day that you still want to quit, that means it is what you really want."

GYMNASTICS IS NOT EVERYTHING

I've just written all about how wonderful, challenging, and life-changing gymnastics is. But it shouldn't be your whole world. It is important to have a well-rounded life, so if you do decide to quit, then you have other things to be excited about. After so many years, gymnastics can feel like your whole identity—but it shouldn't. Gymnastics is what you do; it's not who you are. There are so many things you are capable of.

Dr. Alison Arnold, MS, PhD (Doc Ali), says that "if you do feel that it is time to leave the sport, then let your joy lead. Think about what brings you joy, and that should be where you go next. Don't make your decision based on a bad day or bad week; it should be after thinking and meditating on it, listening to your heart and then coming to a solution. If it is time, remember to take the amazing gifts that the sport has given you: teamwork, overcoming obstacles, confidence, etc. Look back and remember everything you've learned, and use those as you go into the next thing, whatever that thing may be."

The decision to let go of something you've been working on for much of your life is not a simple or easy one. Before you think negatively of yourself for being a "quitter," realize that you may have other incredible talents and passions that you simply have not been able to realize! Trust your gut and take everything you've learned from the sport and apply it to your next venture.

Gymnastics is tough and will put you through countless ups and downs. You have probably heard the quip, "If gymnastics were easy, then it would be called football." I have nothing against football but it's true! There is no sport quite like gymnastics, for all the good and bad reasons listed in this book. Whatever you choose, you will be a better athlete and person for having a gymnastics background. I guarantee it.

CHAPTER 12 KEY TAKEAWAYS

1. Staying or leaving gymnastics is an extremely difficult decision.

2. If you are not ready to quit, but aren't enjoying gymnastics, try taking a step back from the intensity of training; stay present where you are now rather than thinking about the "what ifs" of the future; gamify practice to make it less serious and more fun; take the pressure off yourself; and take a breather to enjoy some time off.

3. If you want to stay involved in gymnastics in a less intense way, the Xcel track is a great alternative that is less competitive and requires less of a time commitment.

4. If your heart isn't in gymnastics, also remember that it is okay to quit. You shouldn't be spending all your time and energy on something that you don't love anymore. There are other sports and experiences out there waiting for you.

5. Gymnastics is a wonderful sport, but it also isn't everything. Take what you've learned from the sport and use it to make you a better person and athlete in whatever you decide to do next.

CHAPTER 13

FOR THE PARENTS

If you are like my parents and many other parents, no one provided you with a guidebook on being the parent of a gymnast. Leotards, sparkly hair, choreographed routines, road trips, carpools, grips, and Tiger Paws: I'm sure you didn't anticipate this world of gymnastics that somehow your child is now a part of. I'm guessing you simply put your kid in gymnastics classes because you wanted them to be healthy, be active, and have a passion. Now, after the countless hours in the gym, money you've spent, and friends you've seen your child make, they tell you that they don't want to do gymnastics anymore. Where do you go from here? You could be the parent who immediately accepts their child's wishes or the parent who insists that nothing worth having comes easy, and they need to stick it out.

I first want to say that your child bringing up thoughts of quitting is completely normal. I would think it strange if they didn't! Just as with any recreational activity, some days are great and some not so much. If there are a lot of not-so-great days for an extended period, then your child may be starting to talk about quitting. What are you supposed to do? You've never had to deal with this before. Do you let them quit right then and there? Tell them they absolutely cannot? Or make them wait until the end of the season? There is no easy choice. The first thing I suggest is simply to listen to their reasoning and really try to hear what they are saying objectively. Their reasons could be not having a good practice, fear of a skill or event, an injury, or not liking their teammates or coaches. There are many other possibilities. Hear them out and give your loving but objective thoughts. And keep checking in. It could be just a bad day or bad week, or it could be something that they've been thinking about for a long time.

IF THEY STILL WANT TO QUIT...

If after discussion they still want to quit, then there are other solutions. For example, there are other, less intense options (discussed in chapter 12), which allow your child to stay in the sport, but with less of a time commitment (and less expense for you). The Xcel program or another program, depending on your state (see page 177), offers a great way to stay involved in gymnastics with slightly different rules. Not all gyms have an Xcel team, so ask what your gym offers. Rather than levels, Xcel is made up of divisions, which are usually less intense and allow your child to still compete but on a less rigorous scale. The time commitment Xcel requires is also less than that of a development track team. Gymnasts do not have to compete in all the events. Instead, they can specialize in an event or two and not compete in the others (similar to college gymnastics). It is even possible to do Xcel and then later participate in development track; it may just take a little backtracking.

Additionally, if your child wants to stay at the same gym but not do gymnastics, then most gyms offer trampoline or tumbling classes, which include many similar aspects of artistic gymnastics.

If the coaches or teammates are the issue, then you could try another gym. There may be one or two people at the gym now who make your kid's life a headache, so being around a new group of people could be the answer.

If the problem is fear, then going back a level might solve the problem. Maybe your child is feeling too much pressure to compete at their current level. Taking a few steps back or not moving to the next level could be a good way to build up their confidence until they are ready for the next step. I repeated both levels 8 and 9 twice until I was mentally ready and had the skills to compete at level 10.

Fears are a completely normal and a very common part of gymnastics. It's difficult as a parent to watch your child struggle as they navigate this. You may want to offer advice on how to overcome their fear or try to talk about it to make your child feel better. Only you know how your child will receive this. Don't get drawn into long conversations about why they have this fear, what can be done, or your suggestions. Allow them to bring it up on their own, and let them voice their thoughts. You should acknowledge that what they are doing is scary and offer encouragement for them to "keep trying" and to "trust your training; this skill will come eventually." As frustrating as it is for you, there is nothing you can do to solve this problem for them. And even if they overcome this fear, they are almost guaranteed to have another fear waiting and then another after that! Fear is a continuous part of the sport. Only they can figure out how to work through their fears and learn a different skill, or if fear will be the reason that they leave the sport.

If your child doesn't think they are good enough, or if they have been struggling even after repeating a level, then there is also the option for private lessons. Unfortunately, private lessons can be costly, but it may take only a few lessons to make a big difference. If private coaching is out of the question, then either you or your child could have a conversation with the coaches and ask them if improvements in particular areas would help your child succeed. If they need to improve their strength, flexibility, or cardio, these are all things that can be done outside the gym, on their own time.

If your child complains that they have no time to spend with their friends outside the gym, are there any things in their schedule that could be taken out? If not, unfortunately, then there is no getting around this one. The nature of gymnastics is that it is incredibly time-consuming (see chapter 7) and that is part of the sacrifice of the sport.

If you've looked at all the options and your child still insists on leaving gymnastics, then there are other sports that have a lot of overlap with gymnastics. Many gymnasts transition to diving, dance, pole vaulting, cheer, acrobatics and tumbling, rock climbing, and more. In addition to these sports, which are an easy transition from gymnastics, the fitness, strength, flexibility, body and spatial awareness, as well as life lessons learned in gymnastics, translate extremely well to almost any other sport (see chapter 2). More recently, many gymnasts have turned to American Ninja Warrior gyms or CrossFit gyms, which also align well with gymnastics. American Ninja Warrior gyms have different obstacle courses, which include a lot of upper body strength challenges. Gymnasts already have that upper body strength and are often very successful at the ninja warrior training and competitions. CrossFit has also grown significantly over the past few years. This program pushes you to have cross-functional fitness, which also includes many gymnastics movements, such as handstands, handstand walks, handstand pushups, pullovers, leg lifts, levers, rope climbs, parallettes, and rings.

In the end, the skills, coordination, friendships, and life lessons (not to mention all the other positive aspects of gymnastics discussed in this book) gained through the sport will be enough to make your child successful in other sports. I know it is frustrating from a parent's perspective because you are the one who paid for this expensive sport; drove them to practices, competitions, and sleepovers; and saw how much confidence and joy the sport brought to your child. It is difficult not to dwell on these thoughts, but you also don't want a miserable child who is forced to practice and train for a sport that their heart isn't in any longer.

IF THEY STAY

If your child decides that they do in fact want to stay in gymnastics, I unfortunately am here to tell you that these thoughts of quitting will resurface. As I mentioned previously, I had a full-ride scholarship waiting for me and *still* seriously considered quitting. It is normal and part of the sport because it is so demanding and time-consuming at such a pivotal age. Remaining positive, encouraging the growth mindset, and making sure your child stays intrinsically motivated are the best ways to keep them in the sport. Also, remember that it should be their choice (with your guidance) about staying or quitting.

One of the main reasons I stayed in the sport was that my parents didn't try to push me one way or the other. If I talked about quitting, then they would listen and say, "Okay, if that's what you really want." Sometimes they'd say, "Give it just one more week, and then we can have a discussion about it." By the time the end of the week came, I'd have already decided I wanted to stay. This worked for me but you know your child best. How you speak to them about this depends on their personality and your relationship with them.

It's not only important that you as the parent are involved with your child's gymnastics, but also that you stay a parent. Daniel Miranda shares that Gotham Gymnastics has a family support program to educate parents and help them understand their role in their gymnast's life. This allows the coaches to coach (and not parent) and allows the parents to parent (and not coach). They have seen that this program creates better communication and that parents and coaches work better together. Everyone is on the same page, and everyone is a member of a *team*.

CHAPTER 14

GYMNASTICS SCHOLARSHIPS

If continuing gymnastics and earning a scholarship is the route you're hoping to take, then there are a few things to know. These are pointers and facts that I wish I had known when I was going through this process.

WOMEN'S ATHLETIC SCHOLARSHIPS

First, you should know that for women's gymnastics in college there are three divisions: Divisions I, II, and III. In Division I, there are 12 scholarships per team, which are all full scholarships, covering 100 percent of tuition, room, board, and so on. In this case, the scholarship is all-or-nothing. At the Division II level, however, there are six scholarships, and they can be spread out to as many athletes as the coach wants. This means that more athletes can receive at least partial scholarships. At the Division III level, there are no athletic scholarships, but coaches can assist athletes in getting academic aid or grants.

WHAT ARE COACHES LOOKING FOR?

In college gymnastics, most everyone has reached level 10, if not elite. This means that college coaches generally recruit gymnasts who have competed level 10 for at least a year, although many compete level 10 for multiple years. There can be exceptions to competing at level 10, particularly at Division II or III schools. Not only should you compete in level 10, but also college coaches look for athletes who place well at the regional and national competitions. At nationals, there is always a long table for gymnastics coaches who watch and look for new recruits. Many of the athletes who compete at the top gymnastics universities have competed at the elite level.

There are a few ways to start getting college coaches to notice you. Most programs have online questionnaires on their athletic website to start with. Coaches also look at online recruiting videos and follow scores at national competitions. If a coach is interested, then they may invite you to attend their college camp. Even if you weren't personally invited, attending college camps is a great way to see how you like the coaches and the team. You can also personally reach out to the coaches and keep them updated with videos, skills, and scores. It always felt extremely intimidating having to talk to coaches, but it is all part of the process. The biggest thing is getting on their radar.

In addition to athletics, college coaches take academics into consideration. Most universities look at GPA in addition to SAT or ACT scores. Some universities are getting rid of standard testing requirements, so be sure to check. The National Collegiate Athletic Association (NCAA) sets academic requirements to be considered for Division I scholarships. These requirements include the following:[70]

- You must graduate high school.
- You must complete 16 NCAA-approved core courses (four years of English, three years of math [algebra or higher], two years of science, one extra year of either English, math, or science, two years of social science, and four years of other areas, such as world languages, comparative religions, philosophy, and so on).
- You must complete 10 of your 16 core courses before your seventh semester (senior year), including seven in English, math, or natural/ physical sciences. Once you begin your seventh semester, you may not repeat or replace any of those 10 courses to improve your core-course GPA.
- You must earn at least a 2.3 GPA in your core courses, which are outlined in the NCAA academic requirements.

You can check the NCAA Division I Academic Standards page[71] to stay up-to-date with these requirements.

HOW TO IMPROVE YOUR CHANCES

1. Connect with college coaches: The best way to connect with college coaches is to contact them online first. This means creating recruiting videos that show your skills and abilities. Once you pique the interest of a coach, they may scout you out at competitions or camps, but to get their attention in the first place, you need to demonstrate what you can do. As already noted, almost all college teams have recruiting questionnaires where you fill out your contact information, academic information (high school GPA, academic honors, and college counselor contact information), your coach's contact information, statistics for your current season, career statistics, and skills.

2. Attend college gymnastics camps: Many of the top gymnastics programs hold summer camps. Some camps are open to anyone, and some are by invitation only. This is a great way to interact with current gymnasts on the team, as well as be recognized by college coaches.

3. Have an online athletic recruiting profile: One of the most challenging aspects of getting recruited is being found. If you have an athletic recruiting profile that includes your academic and athletic achievements, coaches will be able to get most of the information they need in one place.

4. Be strong in several events: College coaches will generally recruit an athlete who is successful at multiple events. Once you get to college, you will specialize in the events that you are best at. For some people, this is competing all-around, but for many people it is competing in just one or two events.

5. Talk to your club coach: It makes sense that college coaches want to talk to your current coach to ask what kind of athlete and person you are. College coaches want to hear how you perform under pressure and if you have any underlying injuries. Speak with your current coach to make sure they are talking you up over the phone and at meets with college coaches.

RECRUITING RULES

There are specific rules and terms regarding recruiting that must be followed by the gymnast, their family, and college coaches. Following are some important terms,[72] and then we will get into timing and rules.

Contact: A coach interacting with you or your parents off the college campus.

Verbal commitment: A verbal statement that you will compete for a university. This is nonbinding and can be made at any time.

Official visit: When the university pays for you, your parents, or all of you to visit the university. This covers transportation to and from campus, lodging, three meals a day, and reasonable entertainment expenses, including three tickets to a home sporting event.

Unofficial visit: You can set up an unofficial visit and visit a school anytime on your own dime. The only thing a school could pay for is three tickets to a home sporting event.

National letter of intent (NLI): This is a binding agreement between you and a university. You need to sign an NLI only if you are receiving a scholarship. Once it is signed, the student agrees to attend that school for at least one academic year, and the school agrees to pay the scholarship for at least one academic year. Once a student-athlete signs an NLI, it ends the recruiting process for them. If a student signs an NLI but attends another school, then they lose one year of eligibility (they cannot compete for a full year). Athletes often choose to sign because it finalizes the agreement between the athletes and the school.

RECRUITMENT DATES

Anytime

Coaches can reach out to athletes and their families with general recruiting materials, such as camp brochures and questionnaires; however, this is the only contact allowed before the dates that follow. It's also worth noting that you (or a member of your family) is allowed to reach out to college coaches to send videos or updates, but coaches are not allowed to respond.

June 15

On June 15 after your sophomore year of high school, coaches are allowed to call or email you. Coaches can even make verbal offers on this date.

For Division II schools: You are allowed to make official and unofficial visits to Division II universities.

August 1

For Division I: On August 1 of your junior year of high school, you can start making official and unofficial visits to Division I colleges.

Mid-November

Mid-November of your junior year of high school is when you sign your NLI to officially commit to a university (that is, scholarship offers are finalized). The exact date in November varies from year to year.

You can delay signing if you are waiting on other offers. You have between mid-November of your senior year and August 1 of the following year to commit.

For example, if you are graduating in 2025, then you would sign between mid-November 2024 and August 1, 2025. For the exact dates (based on the date of your high school graduation and the date you begin college), refer to www. nationalletter.org/signingDates.

DIVISION III

The NCAA allows Division III coaches more flexibility with recruiting because these coaches cannot offer full athletic scholarships. Division III coaches are allowed to have digital communication with a gymnast at any time and have off-campus contact after a gymnast's sophomore year of high school. Gymnasts can make unofficial visits to Division III schools at any time and can make official visits starting January 1 of their junior year of high school.

WHEN WILL I RECEIVE AN OFFER?

There are specific rules that college coaches must follow in order to stay NCAA-compliant; however, coaches have worked around these rules. For example, even if a college coach can't talk directly to an athlete, that coach is able to reach out to an athlete's club coach at any time. As an athlete, you are allowed to send the college coaches recruiting videos and school transcripts. The college coach just isn't allowed to respond until June of your sophomore year. There are stories of athletes being verbally offered scholarships or spots on teams when they are in eighth or ninth grade, but most are in tenth or eleventh grade. An athlete can make a verbal commitment to a school at any time. Note that a verbal offer from the coach and commitment by the student is nonbinding, and either party can change their mind. The NCAA does not recognize or even track verbal commitments between athletes and colleges.[73] The official (and legal) commitment from both sides comes once the NLI is signed. Although a verbal commitment is nonbinding, it is fairly uncommon for a school to rescind their verbal offer (although not impossible).

WALKING ON

Although a full-ride scholarship is an honor and an accomplishment, at the end of the day you are attending university as a *student*-athlete. Attending a school that aligns with your academic aspirations is critical. You may decide on a college for many reasons, and gymnastics does not have to be the deciding factor! In this case, you may want to attend a university or be on a gymnastics team that doesn't offer you a scholarship or doesn't have any left. What to do next? Because for Division I teams there are only 12 scholarships and on average 18 athletes, some Division I athletes will be offered a walk-on spot. They are full members of the team, but they are without funding. They are just as much a part of the team and get the same swag, or athletic gear, including shirts, sweatshirts, sweatpants, shoes, and so on, as the rest of the team.

RANKINGS

As of August 2024, the Women's NCAA Gymnastics ranking is as follows:[74] It is important to note that these rankings can change significantly year to year!

Rank	Team	Division
1	LSU	I
2	UC Berkeley	I
3	Utah	I
4	Florida	I
5	Stanford	I
6	Oklahoma	I
7	Arkansas	I
8	Alabama	I
9	Kentucky	I
10	Denver	I
11	Missouri	I
12	Minnesota	I
13	Ohio State	I
14	Michigan State	I
15	Penn State	I
16	Arizona State	I
17	UCLA	I
18	Georgia	I
19	Michigan	I
20	Auburn	I
21	Oregon State	I
22	Illinois	I

Rank	Team	Division
23	Washington	I
24	Nebraska	I
25	BYU	I
26	Maryland	I
27	Southern Utah	I
28	North Carolina State	I
29	Iowa State	I
30	Kent State	I
31	Arizona	I
32	Towson	I
33	Boise State	I
34	Ball State	I
35	Clemson	I
36	San Jose State	I
37	Iowa	I
38	George Washington	I
39	Western Michigan	I
40	Central Michigan	I
41	Pittsburgh	I
42	North Carolina	I
43	Lindenwood	I
44	Illinois State	I
45	Utah State	I
46	Rutgers	I
47	UC Davis	I
48	New Hampshire	I

Rank	Team	Division
49	Pennsylvania	I
50	Eastern Michigan	I
51	Texas Women's	II
52	Temple	I
53	West Virginia	I
54	Sacramento State	I
55	Northern Illinois	I
56	Air Force	I
57	Bowling Green	I
58	Yale	I
59	S.E. Missouri	I
60	LIU	I
61	Brown	II
62	West Chester	I
63	William and Mary	I
64	Cornell	II
65	Bridgeport	II
66	Southern Connecticut	II
67	UW–Oshkosh	III
68	Brockport	III
69	UW–La Crosse	III
70	UW–Whitewater	III
71	Fisk	III
72	Alaska	I
73	Talladega	II
74	UW–Stout	III

Rank	Team	Division
75	Cortland State	III
76	Rhode Island College	III
77	Ithaca College	III
78	Ursinus College	III
79	Springfield College	III
80	Centenary College	III
81	UW–Eau Claire	III
82	Winona State	III
83	Greenville	III
84	Gustavus Adolphus	III
85	Utica	III
86	Simpson	III
87	Hamline	III

WOMEN

Division	Number of Teams	Number of Scholarships
Division I	60	12
Division II	5	6
Division III	19	0

MEN

Although there are many similarities in men's and women's gymnastics, there are a few key differences. At the collegiate level, there are only Division I and Division III teams for men. Men's college coaches are looking only for athletes who have competed at level 10. And unfortunately, fewer universities have men's gymnastics. The rankings as of August 2024 are as follows.[75]

Rank	Team	Division
1	Stanford	I
2	Michigan	I
3	Oklahoma	I
4	Nebraska	I
5	Illinois	I
6	Ohio State	I
7	California	I
8	Penn State	I
9	Air Force	I
10	Navy	I
11	Greenville	I
12	Springfield College	III
13	Army	I
14	William and Mary	III
15	Simpson	III

For the most up-to-date team rankings, check out Roadtonationals.com. Stay up-to-date on what the latest preseason polls say, where recruits have committed, who to watch in the next season, and more, at Collegegymnews.com.

I hope you will be able to visit some universities to get a feel for the campus and its academic offerings. Perhaps you can meet the gymnastics coaching staff and maybe even some of the athletes to ask them questions. While you're visiting, try to get a feel for the culture of the team and the atmosphere at practice (if possible). At first, you may be thinking only about the school's gymnastics ranking, but you're going to be in college for the next four years. You want to be somewhere that has a healthy team culture and will provide you with an enjoyable college experience. I've heard horror stories of coaches pitting athletes against each other and ruthless competitiveness between athletes that is highly toxic. You want to find a program that suits your gymnastic ability, helps you grow as an athlete and a person, and still offers you the full college experience. Yes, gymnastics will take a lot of your time, but also think about how you want to spend your time outside the gym and how your university education can help set you up for a job after graduation.

A discussion of the pros and cons of competing at the college level could be an entire book. I will not get into that now, but if you have questions about competing at the collegiate level, then send me an email at jlkonner@gmail .com, talk to anyone you know who has competed in collegiate sport, ask athletes when you visit universities, or go to the summer camps. Just as in club gymnastics, the experiences and friendships in college gymnastics are life-changing. I traveled a bumpy road getting through club and collegiate gymnastics. That said, there is no other sport like gymnastics, and I couldn't be more grateful for what I've gained from it.

ENDNOTES

1 Michele M. Tugade and Barbara L. Fredrickson, "Resilient Individuals Use Positive Emotions to Bounce Back from Negative Emotional Experiences," *Journal of Personality and Social Psychology* 86, no. 2 (2004): 320–33, doi:10.1037/0022-3514.86.2.320.

2 Felix Bittmann, "When Problems Just Bounce Back: About the Relation Between Resilience and Academic Success in German Tertiary Education," SN Social Sciences 1, no. 2 (2021): 65. doi: 10.1007/s43545-021-00060-6.

3 Angela Lee Duckworth, "Grit: The Power of Passion and Perserverance," filmed April 2013 in New York, TED video, 5:59, https://www.ted.com/talks/angela_lee_duckworth_grit_the_power_of_passion_and_perseverance.

4 Angela L. Duckworth et al., "Grit: Perseverance and Passion for Long-Term Goals," *Journal of Personality and Social Psychology* 92, no. 6 (2007): 1087–1101.

5 Clifton B. Parker, "Perseverance Key to Children's Intellectual Growth, Stanford Scholar Says," Stanford, April 19, 2015, https://news.stanford.edu/2015/04/29/dweck-kids-potential-042915.

6 Carol S. Dweck and David S. Yeager, "Mindsets: A View from Two Eras," *Perspectives on Psychological Science* 14, no. 3 (2019): 481–96, https://doi.org/10.1177/1745691618804166.

7 Duckworth, "Grit: The Power of Passion and Perserverance."

8 Karen Cogan, "Mental Toughness in Gymnastics," accessed April 15, 2024, https://static.usagym.org/PDFs/About%20USA%20Gymnastics/wellness/mh_mentaltoughness.pdf.

9 George Hood, "What Is Mental Toughness?" Medium, February 26, 2023, https://teamhoodworldrecords.medium.com/what-is-mental-toughness-fc3839fdf534.

10 "Heather O'Reilly Quotes," BrainyQuote.com, accessed April 15, 2024, https://www.brainyquote.com/quotes/heather_oreilly_425520.

11 Barbara J. Campbell, "Exercise and Bone Health," OrthoInfo.org, July 2020, https://orthoinfo.aaos.org/en/staying-healthy/exercise-and-bone-health.

12 S. J. Fleck and J. E. Falkel, "Value of Resistance Training for the Reduction of Sports Injuries," *Sports Medicine* (Auckland, N.Z.) 3, no. 1 (1986): 61–68, doi:10.2165/00007256-198603010-00006.

13 Heidi Godman, "Is It Too Late to Save Your Posture?," *Harvard Health Publishing*, April 7, 2022, accessed April 15, 2024, www.health.harvard.edu/exercise-and-fitness/is-it-too-late-to-save-your-posture.

14 "10 Benefits of Resistance Training with Isometric Holds," American Sports & Fitness Association, accessed April 15, 2024, www.americansportandfitness.com/blogs/fitness-blog/the-top-10-benefits-of-resistance-training-with-isometric-holds.

15 Brian Tracy, "Eat that Frog: Brian Tracy Explains the Truth about Frogs," BrianTracy.com, accessed April 15, 2024, https://www.briantracy.com/blog/time-management/the-truth-about-frogs.

16 "Core Functions in Leadership," CommunityToolBox.edu, accessed April 15, 2024, https://ctb.ku.edu/en/table-of-contents/leadership/leadership-functions/build-sustain-commitment.

17 "Hardworking Definition & Meaning." Merriam-Webster.

18 Mahin Etemadi Nia and Mohammad Ali Besharat, "Comparison of Athletes' Personality Characteristics in Individual and Team Sports," *Procedia Social and Behavioral Sciences* no. 5 (2010): 808–12.

19 Stephen Duneier, "How to Achieve Your Most Ambitious Goals TEDxTucson," YouTube, March 6, 2017, https://www.youtube.com/watch?v=TQMbvJNRpLE.

20 Donna J. Cech and Suzanne "Tink" Martin, *Functional Movement Development Across the Life Span*, 3rd ed. (St. Louis: Elsevier/Saunders, 2012) page 11.

21 Hayley S. Mountford, Amanda Hill, Anna L. Barnett, and Dianne F. Newbury, "Genome-Wide Association Study of Motor Coordination," *Frontiers in Human Neuroscience*, vol. 15 (June 9, 2021): 669902.

22 Luis Lopes et al., "Associations Between Sedentary Behavior and Motor Coordination in Children," *American Journal of Human Biology: The Official*

Journal of the Human Biology Council 24, no. 6 (2012): 746–52. doi:10.1002/ajhb.22310.

23 "Gross Motor Skills: Birth to 5 Years," Children's Hospital of Richmond, accessed April 15, 2024, https://www.chrichmond.org/services/therapy-services/developmental-milestones/gross-motor-skills-birth-to-5-years.

24 Understood, "Gross Motor Skills vs. Fine Motor Skills: What's the Difference?" YouTube, July 12, 2017, https://www.youtube.com/watch?v=l93BTYyHG0c&t=2s.

25 Strength Matters, "What Is Athleticism? The 10 Components of Complete Athleticism," YouTube, December 13, 2022, https://www.youtube.com/watch?v=8oFsZxN1_ns.

26 Jenny Marder, "Uncoordinated? You Can Still Be an Athlete.," *New York Times*, July 6, 2023, www.nytimes.com/2023/07/06/well/move/clumsiness-coordination-sports-exercise.html.

27 Visualization—The Secret, "Visualization used by Michael Phelps," YouTube, November 2, 2020, https://www.youtube.com/watch?v=3-mm90LFPqU.

28 Marty Durden, "Utilizing Imagery to Enhance Injury Rehabilitation," *The Sport Journal*, accessed April 15, 2024, https://thesportjournal.org/article/utilizing-imagery-to-enhance-injury-rehabilitation.

29 D. Landers, P. McCullagh, R. Nilam, S. Riggs, and S. Skaling, "A Comparison of Modeling and Imagery in the Acquisition and Retention of Motor Skills," *Journal of Sport Science* 25, no. 5 (2006): 587–597.

30 Marty Durden, "Utilizing Imagery to Enhance Injury Rehabilitation."

31 "Confidence," Psychology Today, accessed April 15, 2024, https://www.psychologytoday.com/us/basics/confidence.

32 Don A. Moore, "Perfectly Confident Leadership," *California Management Review* 63, no. 3 (2021): 58–69.

33 Don A. Moore, "Perfectly Confident Leadership."

34 "Comfort Zone," Cambridge Dictionary, accessed April 15, 2024, https://dictionary.cambridge.org/us/dictionary/english/comfort-zone.

35 Paul Jenkins, "Why Confidence Is Important (and How to Boost It)," Brilliantio.com, accessed April 15, 2024, https://brilliantio.com/why-confidence-is-important.

36 Kosuke Sato and Masaki Yuki, "The Association Between Self-Esteem and Happiness Differs in Relationally Mobile vs. Stable Interpersonal Contexts," *Frontiers in Psychology* 5 (2014): 1113. doi:10.3389/fpsyg.2014.01113.

37 US National Science Foundation, accessed April 15, 2024, https://www.nsf.gov.

38 Drew Wilkins, "Developing a Winning Mindset for Success in 2024," PursuePerformance.com, last updated February 19, 2024, https://pursueperformance.com/winning-mindset.

39 Lena Aburdene Derhally, "The Importance of Childhood Friendships, and How to Nurture Them," *The Washington Post*, July 25, 2016, https://www.washingtonpost.com/news/parenting/wp/2016/07/25/the-importance-of-childhood-friendships-and-how-to-nurture-them.

40 Angus Chen, "Having a Best Friend in Your Teenage Years Could Benefit You for Life," NPR, August 26, 2017, https://www.npr.org/sections/health-shots/2017/08/26/543739986/having-a-best-friend-in-your-teenage-years-could-benefit-you-for-life.

41 Millie Ferrer and Anne Fugate, "The Importance of Friendship for School-Age Children," University of Florida, accessed April 15, 2024, https://www.frontierdistrict.k-state.edu/family/child-development/docs/school-age/ImportanceFriendship.pdf.

42 Amy C. Hartl, et al., "Dyadic Instruction for Middle School Students," Learning and Individual Differences (2015): 33–39, https://www.ncbi.nlm.nih.gov/pmc/articles/PMC4681000/#R13.

43 Gregory D. Myer et al., "Sports Specialization, Part II: Alternative Solutions to Early Sport Specialization in Youth Athletes," *Sports Health* 8, no. 1 (2016): 65–73. doi:10.1177/1941738115614811.

44 International Physical Literacy Association, accessed April 15, 2024, https://www.physical-literacy.org.uk.

45 "Oldest Gymnast." Guinness World Records, www.guinnessworldrecords.com/world-records/oldest-gymnast. Accessed April 22, 2024.

46 Lena Smirnova, "From Running on Rooftops to Vaulting into Eight Olympics: How Oksana ChusovitinaWent from Wild Child to Legend," Olympics.com, September 28, 2023, https://olympics.com/en/news/oksana-chusovitina-exclusive-childhood-family-future-paris-2024. Accessed April 22, 2024.

47 Sunjay Nath's LinkedIn Profile, accessed April 24, 2024, https://www.linkedin.com/posts/sunjaynath_i-trained-4-years-to-run-9-seconds-and-people-activity-6878363618023378944-lemJ.

48 Anna Kojac, "Why Your Fearless Gymnast is Suddenly Fearful," StickItGirl. com, accessed April 15, 2024, https://stickitgirl.com/blogs/stickitgirl/why-your-fearless-gymnast-is-all-of-a-sudden-afraid.

49 Qais AbuHasan, Vamsi Reddy, and Waquar Siddiqui, *Neuroanatomy*, Treasure Island, FL: StatPearls Publishing, 2024, https://www.ncbi.nlm.nih.gov/books/ NBK537102.

50 Alice Park, "Simone Biles Has the Twisties. What Are They, and Why Are They So Dangerous?" *TIME*, July 30, 2021, https://time.com/6085776/simone-biles-twisties-gymnastics.

51 Brian Cain, "How to Coach Your Athletes to Use Fear as Fuel," BrianCain.com, accessed April 15, 2024, https://briancain.com/blog/how-to-coach-your-athletes-to-use-fear-as-fuel.html.

52 Scott B. Martin et al., "Worries and Fears Associated with Competitive Gymnastics," *Journal of Clinical Sport Psychology* vol 2, issue 4 (2008): 299–316.

53 "Body Dysmorphic Disorder," Hopkins Medicine, accessed April 15, 2024, https://www.hopkinsmedicine.org/health/conditions-and-diseases/body-dysmorphic-disorder.

54 "Eating Disorders," National Institute of Mental Health, accessed April 15, 2024, https://www.nimh.nih.gov/health/topics/eating-disorders.

55 "Disordered Eating & Dieting," NEDC.com, accessed April 15, 2024, https:// nedc.com.au/eating-disorders/eating-disorders-explained/disordered-eating-and-dieting.

56 Martha Fisburne, "'A Tough Balance': Body Image as a Gymnast," *The Stanford Daily*, July 16, 2020, https://stanforddaily.com/2020/07/16/sports-body-image.

57 Stoeber, J., "Perfectionism and Performance" (2012), in S. M. Murphy (Ed.), *Oxford Handbook of Sport and Performance Psychology* (pp. 294-306),New York: Oxford University Press.

58 OWN, "Why Brené Brown Says Perfectionism Is a 20-Ton Shield," Oprah's Lifeclass, Oprah Winfrey Network," YouTube, October 6, 2013, https://www. youtube.com/watch?v=o7yYFHyvweE.

59 Sarah J. Egan, Tracey D. Wade, and Roz Shafran, "Perfectionism as a Transdiagnostic Process: A Clinical Review," *Clinical Psychology Review* 31, no. 2 (2011): 203–12,

60 Prem S. Fry and Dominique L. Debats, "Perfectionism and the Five-Factor Personality Traits as Predictors of Mortality in Older Adults," *Journal of Health Psychology* 14, no. 4 (2009): 513–24, doi:10.1177/1359105309103571.

61 Sharon Martin, "34 Affirmations for When Perfectionism Makes You Feel Inadequate," PsychCentral.com, May 24, 2019, https://psychcentral.com/blog/imperfect/2019/05/34-affirmations-for-when-perfectionism-makes-you-feel-inadequate#1.

62 "Common Gymnastics Injuries: Treatment and Prevention," UPMC.com, accessed April 15, 2024, https://www.upmc.com/services/sports-medicine/for-athletes/gymnastics.

63 Robert W. Westermann et al., "Evaluation of Men's and Women's Gymnastics Injuries: A 10-Year Observational Study," *Sports Health* 7, no. 2 (2015): 161-5. Doi:10.1177/1941738114559705.

64 Robert W. Westermann et al., "Evaluation of Men's and Women's Gymnastics Injuries: A 10-Year Observational Study."

65 Mary L. Gavin, "Growth and Your 13- to 18-Year-Old," KidsHealth.org, June 2019, https://kidshealth.org/en/parents/growth-13-to-18.html.

66 Zero to Finals, "Understanding Odgood-Schlatter Disease," YouTube, November 9, 2022, https://www.youtube.com/watch?v=AZt21fpR6qQ&t=48s.

67 Davis L. Rogers et al., "How Mental Health Affects Injury Risk and Outcomes in Athletes," *Sports Health* 16, no. 2 (2024): 222—29. Doi:10.1177/19417381231179678.

68 Maamer Slimani et al., "Effects of Mental Imagery on Muscular Strength in Healthy and Patient Participants: A Systematic Review," *Journal of Sports Science and Medicine* 15, no. 3 (2016): 434–50.

69 John List, "Success 2.0: Taking the Leap," Hidden Brain podcast audio, May 1, 2023.

70 "Division I Academic Standards," NCAA, accessed April 15, 2024, http://fs.ncaa.org/Docs/eligibility_center/Student_Resources/DI_ReqsFactSheet.pdf.

71 "NCAA Eligibility Requirements for Student-Athletes." NCSA College Recruiting, accessed April 15, 2024, www.ncsasports.org/ncaa-eligibility-center/eligibility-requirements.

72 "Recruiting Rules," CollegeGymRules.com, accessed April 15, 2024, https://collegegymnews.com/rules-resources-hub/recruiting-rules.

73 "Verbal Offers and Commitments: FAQs and Answers," NCSA Sports, accessed April 15, 2024, https://www.ncsasports.org/recruiting/managing-recruiting-process/verbal-offers-and-commitments.

74 RoadToNationals.com, accessed April 22, 2024, https://roadtonationals.com/results/standings.

75 RoadToNationals.com, accessed April 22, 2024, https://roadtonationals.com/results/standingsM.

ACKNOWLEDGMENTS

I never would have had the opportunity to write this book if it weren't for my agent, and more importantly, my aunt, Linda Konner. Thank you for sometimes having more faith in my writing than me and truly making this incredible experience possible.

To my former teammates and current friends who were willing to share their stories and experiences, with all the good, bad, and confusing memories that come with them. Thank you to Zoe Cheng, Dallas Wolfe, Lauren Schmeiss, and Courteney Merker.

To all my coaches over the years who have forever left a positive impact on my life: Tian Zhang, Suzanne Ryan, Kim Hughes, Randy Solorio, Melissa Genovese, Tanya Ho, and especially, Ken Anderson. Ken went above and beyond as my coach growing up, helping me reach the collegiate gymnastics level, and even today getting photos for the book and promoting it.

Thank you to all the experts who answered my calls and emails to allow me to interview you and gain more professional insight: Daniel Miranda, Cassie Rice, Steven Low, Dr. Lisa Young, Dr. Alison Arnold, and Dr. Nolan Merker.

Kierra Sondereker and the entire team at Ulysses Press and VeloPress: Thank you for making me a better writer and believing in this book. I am grateful for the time and energy that went into making this book happen.

To my always encouraging parents and the kindest person I know, my brother, Scott: You all wonder why I constantly work on five projects at once, but love and support me anyway. This would never have been possible without you. I love and appreciate you.

ABOUT THE AUTHOR

Julia Konner, MPH, CHES, is a former collegiate Division 1 student-athlete and coach with over 16 years of competing as an artistic gymnast. Through her many years as a club athlete, collegiate athlete, and team captain, she has faced her own adversities through injuries, body image issues, and impact that training 30+ hours/week has had on her social life. Over the years she has helped countless young and college-aged athletes navigate the ups and downs of the complicated, arduous, and time-consuming sport of gymnastics. Through her personal experience and intricate knowledge of the sport, Konner provides evidence-based advice for young gymnasts at every level.

Konner holds a master's in public health (MPH) from the University of California, Davis. During and after finishing her graduate work, she worked in research and program management related to prevention and mitigation of chronic diseases through healthier lifestyle habits. She remains active as a competitive CrossFit athlete, focused on both the physical side of strength as well as the mental. She currently lives in Washington, DC, and works in public health. She can be reached at jlkonner@gmail.com.